Physical Characteristics of the Gordon Setter

(from the American Kennel Club breed standard)

Topline: Moderately sloping.

Body: Short from shoulder to hips.

Tail: Short and not reaching below the hocks...thick at the root and finishing in a fine point.

Hindquarters: The hind legs from hip to hock are long, flat and muscular; from hock to heel, short and strong. The stifle and hock joints are well bent and not turned either in or out.

Coat: Soft and shining, straight or slightly waved, but not curly, with long hair on ears, under stomach and on chest, on back of the fore and hind legs, and on the tail.

Height (at shoulder): Males, 24 to 27 inches; females, 23 to 26 inches.

Weight: Males, 55 to 80 pounds; females, 45 to 70 pounds.

Color and Markings: Black with tan markings, either of rich chestnut or mahogany color.

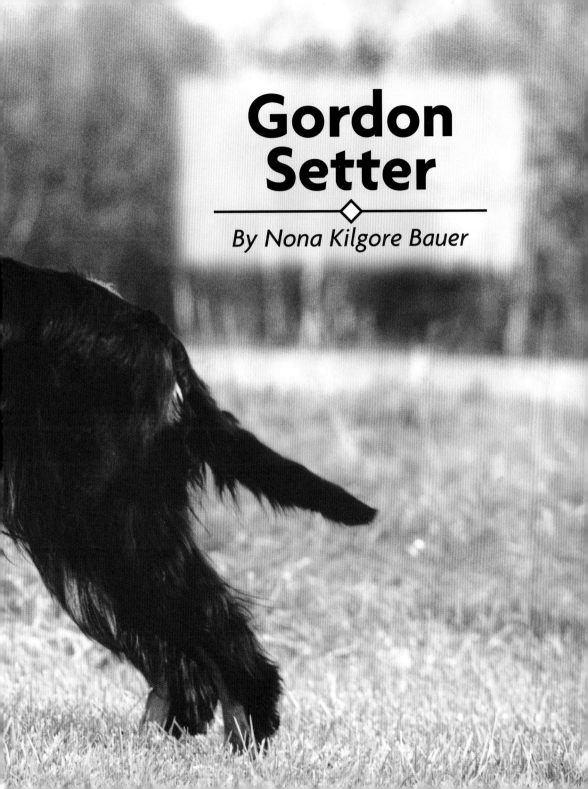

Gordon Setter

◇

By Nona Kilgore Bauer

Contents

Training Your Gordon Setter 80

Begin with the basics of training the puppy and adult dog. Learn the principles of house-training the Gordon Setter, including the use of crates and basic scent instincts. Get started by introducing the pup to his collar and leash and progress to the basic commands. Find out about obedience classes and training for other activities.

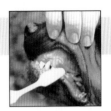

Healthcare of Your Gordon Setter 107

By Lowell Ackerman DVM, DACVD
Become your dog's healthcare advocate and a well-educated canine keeper. Select a skilled and able veterinarian. Discuss pet insurance, vaccinations and infectious diseases, the neuter/spay decision and a sensible, effective plan for parasite control, including fleas, ticks and worms.

Your Senior Gordon Setter 134

Know when to consider your Gordon Setter a senior and what special needs he will have. Learn to recognize the signs of aging in terms of physical and behavioral traits and what your vet can do to optimize your dog's golden years. Consider some advice about saying goodbye to your beloved pet.

Showing Your Gordon Setter 144

Step into the center ring and find out about the world of showing pure-bred dogs. Here are the basics of AKC conformation showing, how shows are organized and what's required for your dog to become a champion. Take a leap into other competitive sports: obedience, agility, tracking, field and hunting events.

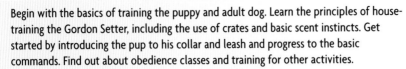

KENNEL CLUB BOOKS® **GORDON SETTER**
ISBN: 1-59378-280-2

Copyright © 2005 • Kennel Club Books, LLC
308 Main Street, Allenhurst, NJ 07711 USA
Cover Design Patented: US 6,435,559 B2 • Printed in South Korea

All rights reserved. No part of this book may be reproduced in any form, by photostat, scanner, microfilm, xerography or any other means, or incorporated into any information retrieval system, electronic or mechanical, without the written permission of the copyright owner.

10 9 8 7 6 5 4 3 2 1

Photography by Carol Ann Johnson
with additional photographs by:

John Ashbey, Paulette Braun, T.J. Calhoun, Cantor Photography, Alan and Sandy Carey, Carolina Biological Supply, Cook Photography, Cott/Francis, David Dalton, Isabelle Français, Gilbert Studios, Bill Jonas, Klein, Dr. Dennis Kunkel, Tam C. Nguyen, Petrulis Studio, Phototake, Jean Claude Revy and Michael Trafford.

Illustrations by Patricia Peters.

The publisher wishes to thank all of the owners whose dogs are illustrated in this book, including Val and Russell Mosedale.

The setter breeds, including the Gordon and the Irish (right), are wonderfully trainable and make responsive family companions.

HISTORY OF THE

GORDON SETTER

Beauty, brains and bird sense.
These glowing accolades describe
the modern Gordon Setter as accu-
rately as they did the "setting" dog
that roamed the highland moors
centuries ago. Those who own the
Gordon Setter would heartily
agree. Although originally developed as a superior working dog
with a distinct tri-color coat, over
the years the Gordon has typically
been kept as a dual-purpose
personal gundog and family
companion known for his black
and tan coloration. It is said that
once you live with a Gordon, you
would own no other breed.

History records the origins of
the Gordon Setter very simply: he
is a native of the hills of bonny
Scotland. Beyond that singular
fact, specific details of his origin
lie hidden in the rolling mists of
his ancestral birthplace.

Early literature suggests the
existence of black-and-tan setters
as far back as the 15th century in
Scotland and England. The early
setter breeds are believed to have
evolved from the first spaniel dogs
whose name reflects their own
country of origin. Spaniels (or
"Spanyells" as they were called
during the era of Henry VIII) took

their name from Spain, long
considered the homeland of the
spaniel that later found its way to
England, France and Ireland.

These original spaniels and
setters were essential to the
survival of their owners. Used in
tandem with hawks to procure
food for the table, they were a
most important asset in areas
where geese and other food-source
birds were plentiful. In those early
days, the dog would couch, or
"set," to indicate the position of
the game birds. On command, the
dog would flush the bird, and the
hawk was immediately released to
capture the prey and bring it back.
In a second method called
"netting," the gamekeeper threw a
net over the flushed birds, a
system that allowed him to assess
the quarry and release the younger
birds to continue their breeding
cycle. Both methods of bird hunting eventually fell from favor with
the advent of the shotgun.

Breeding programs in that era
were based on the talents of the
individual dog rather than on the
promotion of a specific variety or
breed. In her 1620 writing,
*Hunger's Prevention or the Whole
Art of Fowling by Land and Water,*

Young Lorne was the type of Gordon Setter admired in 1878. He is poorly marked and lacks symmetry by today's standards.

A drawing from 1800, believed to be the first well-drawn example of setter breed types. At the top is a Gordon Setter; in the center, an Irish Setter; and reclining, an English Setter.

author Gervaine Markham describes a "setting dog" of the black and fallow (tan) variety as being the "hardest to endure labor," an apt description of the Gordon Setter, who is well known for his endurance as well as his aristocratic coloring. A full century later, in the 1726 *Treatise on Field Diversion*, we read again of "two distinct tribes of setters": the "black and tanned, and the orange, lemon and white."

Despite the myriad accounts and other colorful myths

surrounding the setting dogs of those ancient times, credit for the Gordon Setter is most commonly accorded to a nobleman named Alexander, the Fourth Duke of Gordon (1743–1827).

History's first mention of the Gordon breed refers to the duke's passion for the black-and-tan setter as a gundog of importance. The duke employed a shepherd

who owned a black-and-tan (some accounts say black-and-white) Collie bitch named Maddie who was reputed to be a superb grouse dog, pointing stiffly with her head and tail outstretched. The duke allegedly bred the Collie to his personal setters, although there is no written documentation to prove that the duke deserves such breeding credits. These matings produced dogs with superior noses that tended to circle their

At the turn of the 20th century, the noted canine artist Richard Ansdell painted a setter holding a grouse.

Although not noted for their speed, the dogs had excellent staying power and could press on from morning until nightfall. As hunting dogs, they were easy to break and naturally backed well. Their noses were reputed to be top drawer and they seldom made a false point.

Much of this early history is conjecture, as formal pedigrees were then unknown and records loosely kept at best. Dogs, especially hunting varieties, were bred primarily for their talents and secondarily for an individual breeder's preference for a certain color or ability. Dogs were

An excellent head from 1930, Eng. Ch. Dawn of Daven out of the famous dam Babs of Crombie.

quarry and place the birds between themselves and the gun, much as the Scottish sheepdog circles the flock.

Another nobleman, Lord Rosalyn, who had setters with similar bloodlines, was said to have bred his dogs to the strain created by the duke. Other breedings with alleged Bloodhound crosses further cemented the Gordon's superior scenting powers and his rich black-and-tan coloration.

The mid-nineteenth-century book *The Dogs of Scotland* comments further on the duke's Gordon Castle setter dogs, describing a mostly black-and-tan dog with a heavy ponderous appearance, spaniel-type ears, strong legs and feet, a luxurious well-feathered coat and a regal head.

CANIS LUPUS

"Grandma, what big teeth you have!" The gray wolf, a familiar figure in fairy tales and legends, has had its reputation tarnished and its population pummeled over the centuries. Yet it is the descendants of this much-feared creature to which we open our homes and hearts. Our beloved dog, *Canis domesticus*, derives directly from the gray wolf, a highly social canine that lives in elaborately structured packs. In the wild, the gray wolf can range from 60 to 175 pounds, standing between 25 and 40 inches in height.

Peter of Crombie, the sire of many important champions, was painted by the canine artist Ward Binks in 1928.

frequently offered as gifts to monarchs and other royalty and rulers, which led to further crosses to the more common spaniel and setter strains. Duke Alexander is known to have used setters from other prominent kennels in his breedings, always looking to produce excellent working dogs and improve his breeding stock. It was also known that he preferred the tri-colored coat of black, tan and white because it showed up better on the moors.

When Alexander died in 1827, his estate passed to his eldest heir, George, who, as the Fifth Duke of Gordon, apparently did not share his father's passion for breeding a superior hunting or pointing dog. When George passed away nine years later, the Gordon estate passed this time to a nephew, the Duke of Richmond, who later held the combined title of the Duke of Richmond and Gordon.

During George's reign as duke, the Gordon kennels dwindled to a mere eleven dogs. These remaining dogs were offered at a public sale upon his death in 1836. In what was to become a saving effort, the new heir to Gordon Castle purchased a 5-year-old male named Juno for 34 guineas. Most historical accounts claim that the new duke continued breeding setters of the tri-colored variety. Under 3 generations of nobility, Castle Gordon setter breeding continued for well over 100 years.

Upon the final closing of the Castle kennel in 1907, gundog fancier Isaac Sharpe purchased the remaining Castle setters. Sharpe raised Gordons under the Stylish Gundog prefix, and his records indicate that these were all tri-colored, with black, tan and white markings.

In 1859 canine history took a major step forward with the advent of the first-ever dog show, held at Newcastle on Tyne. Entries were limited to only setters, known then as Black-and-Tans. A Gordon Setter took first prize, a dog named Dandy who was owned by Mr. Jobling. Four years later, at the first field trial ever held for dogs, Gordon Setters also captured first, second and third placements.

With the founding of England's Kennel Club in 1873, the Gordon Setter was classified as a "Black and Tan Setter." As a point of interest, the breed was recognized as the Gordon Setter first by the American Kennel Club in 1892, then three decades later by The Kennel Club in 1923. However, the Gordon had such a devoted following that Gordon Setter breed clubs were founded in the United States in 1888 and in England in 1891, many years before the breed's official recognition in England by The Kennel Club.

The next documented era in the Gordon's history enters the

mid to late 1800s and revolves around devoted British Gordon fancier, the Reverend T. Pearce of Morden Vicarage in Dorset. Rev. Pearce was widely respected in the whole of the canine community and in Gordons in particular. His most famous male, Eng. Ch. Kent of Castle Stock, was widely used at stud, and his influence is still evident in many current Gordon Setter families. Kent reportedly serviced about 60 bitches every year, a stout figure of activity for any male of that time. Kent's most famous progeny resulted from his mating with Rev.

Bydand Coronach, bred by Murray Stewart, became an English champion in 1932.

Pearce's Eng. Ch. Regent, who was out of Lord Bolingbroke's Argyle. The most famous of those whelped included Young Kent, Eng. Ch. Rex, Silk and La Reine.

Rev. Pearce was also a celebrated author who wrote under the pseudonym "Idstone." His writings attributed great brilliance and sensitivity to his Gordons, and he often wrote of their near-human perceptions of his thoughts and needs. In one especially poignant story, Pearce speaks of his Gordon bitch named Rhine. Rhine was a quiet and gentle soul who never fussed about in her kennel, except when she saw Pearce preparing for a shoot. At any indication, she would climb over her 8-foot fence and sneak unseen into his vehicle, often remaining unnoticed until

Bred by Murray Stewart, this is Bydand Clansman, born in 1928.

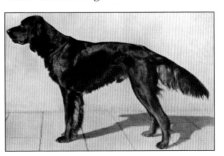

Representing a Continental version of the Gordon in the 1930s, Int. Ch. Lucky was the toast of Dordrecht, Holland. Outstanding for his head, legs and feet, Lucky was bred by J. J. Ambags.

> **GIVE ME MOOR!**
> The Gordon Setter was especially popular as a shooting dog on the Scottish grouse moors, where his strength and stamina were both necessary and advantageous.

the shooters reached their field. On one occasion, she followed her master's scent for over four miles and finally met up with him at his gunning station, thus proving the prowess of the Gordon Setter's nose.

Another of Rev. Pearce's Gordons, Robin, also showed his intelligence and sensitivity while out hunting with a young and inexperienced retriever. The young dog had missed a wounded bird and was struggling in his hunt to find it. Robin was told to stay. Unable to control himself, Robin broke position, found and caught the bird, took it to the younger dog and then returned to his original position. Pearce marveled at the dog's decision to give the bird to the other dog and not to his master, a feat that would stun dog trainers even today. He once wrote of his Gordons, "I myself have had setters of marvellous sagacity...whose reflections and method and deductions have startled me at times, and who acted from a power to which I should hesitate to give the name of instinct."

Despite Rev. Pearce's devotion to the Gordon, it was Isaac Sharpe who raised the Gordon Setter to prominence during the early 20th century. That era witnessed a rise in sport shooting and a demand for dogs to shoot over on a hunt. Isaac Sharpe had acquired the last of the Castle Gordon Setters and kept them under his Stylish Gundog prefix along with other working breeds, such as pointers, spaniels and retrievers, hiring them out for shooting parties by the week and often for an entire hunting season. He also kept a staff of gamekeepers and trainers to accommodate those sportsmen who wanted handlers with the dogs they hired.

Sharpe's Gordons were known to hold their own against the best, whether shooting or running in competition. His famous Gordon, Stylish Ranger, won The Kennel Club Derby in 1901, and The Kennel Club All-Age Stake the following year. Considered the finest Gordon running in his day, Ranger was shipped to Norway in 1906 to continue his breeding career.

Isaac Sharpe's Gordon Setters dominated the breed throughout his lifetime. In 1938, more than 30 years after Ranger was exported, a fine young bitch named Stylish Stagestruck won the Challenge Certificate (a British show award) at England's largest show, Crufts. Again due to

Blossom, tracing her pedigree back to the famous Eng. Ch. Kent of Castle Stock, was bred by Rev. Macdona in 1872. This is a famous painting from the end of the 19th century.

international demand, Stagestruck also left the country when she was purchased by Mrs. Sherman Hoyt of Blakeen kennels in the United States.

The Gordon enjoyed success in both the show ring and the field in the UK. Gradually, however, the true hunter became removed from shows and field trials, and the Gordon Setter fell out of favor. Additionally, some breeders were concerned about the Gordon's size during his development in the late 19th century, contending that he was too big and could not keep pace with the smaller, racier English Setter. And although the Gordon was unequaled in game-finding ability, the breed also suffered due simply to the numerical superiority of the English Setter breed. *The Field Dog Stud Book* for 1902 showed approximately 1200 English Setters registered compared to only 20 Gordons.

Eng. Ch. Bouncer of Ardale, bred by M. Milburn, Jr., became a champion in 1929.

Today's Gordon Setter is family friend and potential hunter dressed in stylish black and tan.

Apparently size was not the only determining factor in the Gordon's decline in popularity. By 1952, one published writing referred to the breed as a "collection piece." Ironically, the breed's failing popularity may have actually saved the Gordon from the exploitation that has plagued other very popular breeds. Compared to popular gundogs like Labrador and Golden Retrievers, the Gordon Setter is generally a healthy breed and prone to only a few of the many health problems common to sporting dogs of similar heritage.

GORDON SETTERS IN THE US

The first Black and Tan Setters to come to the United States were imported from Gordon Castle by George Blunt of New York in 1842; their names were Rake and Rachel, and the latter was given to the famous orator Daniel Webster.

Rake was described as having a white curly coat with tan markings and a black saddle. Rachel was black and tan. Blunt and Webster bred the dogs and used them for hunting, thus establishing the breed on American soil.

In 1874 in Memphis, Tennessee, the first field trial took place, and the dogs entered were recorded as being "setters." These trials, however, didn't take off with Gordon owners, as their dogs did not excel as well as the other gundog breeds. As interest in field trials expanded into the southern and western states, Gordons fell out of favor to the Pointer and English Setter, who could work faster and harder for hours on end.

A hunter and breeder by the name of Harry Malcolm deserves mention for his promotion of the Black and Tan Setters. His large kennel in Maryland did much to put the breed on the map in the East. He served as the first president of the Gordon Setter Club of

EFFECTS OF WAR

World War II was greatly responsible for the current canine gene pool in the UK. Food rationing severely depleted food supplies, and many owners were forced to give up or destroy their dogs. By the end of the six-year war, Gordon Setter numbers were depleted and breeding stock was scarce, limited to many of the dogs seen in modern pedigrees.

America, the organization he founded, and he wrote the first breed standard. In 1877, at the first Westminster Kennel Club Dog Show, 79 Gordon Setters were entered. The American Kennel Club officially changed the breed's name to Gordon Setter in 1892 in honor of the breed's British origins.

During the last quarter of the 19th century, many wealthy American enthusiasts imported outstanding Gordons from England. The British sold many fabulous dogs to American fanciers, and these dogs were consistently winning at the shows. Nevertheless, the first two decades of the new century were a low point for the breed, likely caused by financial woes of the wealthy and the beginning of wildlife conservation laws that impacted hunting.

The revival of the Gordon Setter took place in 1920, thanks to Charles T. Inglee of Inglehurst kennels, who imported stock from Norway, Denmark and Sweden after failing to find enough good-quality dogs in the States. These Scandinavian imports were excellent hunters with strong, racy bodies and dark coloration. Inglehurst Joker became a champion in 1922 and would be the key sire for Mr. Inglee's kennel. Superb in the field and in the show ring, Joker passed along his excellent features in 78 breedings to 300 puppies, 20 of which

> **FIRST AKC GORDON**
> The first Black and Tan Setter to be registered by the National American Kennel Club (later the American Kennel Club) was Bang, whelped in 1875 and owned by J.W. White.

became champions, not the least of whom was Inglehurst Joker Jr. Ch. Petra, Joker Jr.'s dam, produced almost half of Joker's champion get, including Am./Can. Ch. Leitchvale Marksman and Inglehurst Marie, both of which were top winners.

In all, Mr. Inglee bred 300 Gordon litters, producing 40 conformation champions and countless superb hunting dogs, all in his kennel's mere 15 years of operation. Various kennels spun off from Inglehurst, including Dr. Rixford's Rixford kennel, Donald Fordyce's Clonmellerslie kennel and James Munn's Gregorach kennel, the latter producing the group-winning male Ch. Ginger, sire of seven champions.

In 1924 the Gordon Setter Club of America was restarted by Mr. Inglee and six other gentlemen. He held the title of secretary from 1924 until 1929, while Frank Burke was the first president and Hugh MacLaughlin the first treasurer of the reorganized club. With membership in the AKC, the new club began holding specialty shows, field trials and other performance tests.

Dr. A.P. Evans's Svane kennels, also based on Inglehurst dogs, began in 1922 and produced many excellent field trial winners, including Svane June, whose dam was Inglehurst Lady, and Svane Baby June, the daughter of Svane June. The Marcella kennels of James Powell and Frank Morgan also produced dogs of excellent quality, including Ch. Marcella's Bud (sired by Dr. Inglee's Joker) and Ch. Larrabee's Pietro, out of Stylish Fannie.

Other important early kennels were Marinero, owned by John Taafe, and Royal Hall, owned by Pat Hall (both of California); Avalon kennels of A.N. Nichter (Ohio); EEG/Scotia owned by Charles and Edna Girardot (New York); Serlway kennels, owned by Dr. Claude Searle (Illinois); and Blakeen kennels, owned by Mrs. Sherman Hoyt.

Mrs. Girardot based her kennels on Ch. Larrabee's Pietro, bred by the Marcella kennels, and

Ch. Downside Bonnie of Serlway, shown winning Best of Breed at the great Morris & Essex Kennel Club.

Dochfour Beauty, an English import to Avalon kennels. They produced Mrs. Girardot's most famous and first bitch champion, Ch. Larrabee's Avalon Beauty, who produced Ch. EEG's Scotia Nodrog Rettes. Nodrog would become the foundation of the Afternod kennels. Other important dogs here were EEG's Scotia Lancer, Ch. Scotia Lancer's Son, Ch. EEG's Scotia Atom Bomb and Ch. Larrabee's Jock. The EEG Gordons lasted nearly two decades, well into the 1950s.

The Serlway kennels, based in Chicago, were active for only a short period but would have a lasting impact on the breed, providing foundation stock for many East Coast kennels. Beginning with the great stud dog named Bonnie, Dr. Searle's dogs produced many champions. Both Downside Bonnie of Serlway, the sire of 8 champions and the top-winning Gordon since Joker, and Valiant Nutmeg of Serlway, the dam of a record 12 champions, were imported from England. Other important dogs were Ch. Brutus of Serlway (the sire of Ebony Sultan, the second Field Trial Champion), Ch. Black Rogue of Serlway (the sire of Loch Ridge Major Rogue), Ch. Kent of Serlway and Ch. Lancer of Serlway (the sire of Ch. EEG's Scotia Nodrog Rettes).

In the dawn of World War II, British breeders, having learned a hard lesson from World War I, exported their very best dogs to the US in an effort to preserve their lines. Imported in 1936 by Mrs. J. W. Griess, Barnlake Brutus of Salmagundi sired four champions (out of Dr. Searle's Nutmeg) and eight out of Ch. Larrabee's Cricket.

The Heslop kennels were founded by George and Myrtle Heslop in 1936 with Larrabee's Cricket (out of Inglehurst Lady Belle), who also was bred to Brutus to produce two top winners and sires: Courageous and Crusader. Crusader sired a fabulous bitch in Ch. Heslop's Burnvale Duchess, who was bred back to her uncle Courageous several times. Duchess is credited with 13 champion get. The Heslop Gordons provided foundation stock for a number of kennels, including Muriel Clement's Gordon Hill kennels, Margaret Sanger's Sangerfield kennels and Jake and Dottie Poisker's Windy Hill kennels. By the time the Heslops retired in the late 1940s, they had produced 29 champions, a truly remarkable record considering that they did so during the dire times of World War II. Few other kennels were producing dogs or finishing champions during the war.

George Thompson of Baltimore, Maryland started his Loch Ridge kennel in 1940 and continued until the mid 1950s. Thompson based his kennel on

Ch. Sangerfield Portrait, born in 1967, finished her championship at just over a year of age, bred and owned by Fred Itzenplitz.

many fabulous dogs that he purchased from top American breeders, including Mrs. Hoyt, George Heslop and Mrs. Girardot. He bred Loch Ridge Liza Jane (a Brutus-Cricket puppy) to Downside Bonnie to produce Ch. Loch Ridge Dalnaglar Jane and Loch Ridge Vagabond King. The top stud dogs here were Ch. Blakeen Talisman, Loch Ridge Major Rogue (out of Ch. Rita of Avalon CD) and Eng./Am. Ch. Great Scot of Blakeen. The bitches of special note were Ch. Blakeen Saegryte, the dam of seven champions, and Heslop's Dorvius, a top show dog. A Loch Ridge dog, by Talisman out of Saegryte, became the breed's first Dual Champion in 1952. Her name was Dual Champion Loch Ridge Saegryte's Tibby, owned by George Penterman of Shuriridge kennels.

The Milestone kennel of Miriam Steyer Mincieli of the

Ch. Legend of Gael, CD, the top-winning Gordon Setter of 1969, 1970 and 1971, shown with handler Jane Kamp (now Forsyth) at the Ladies Kennel Club in 1971. Legend was owned by Mrs. Cheever Porter.

Bronx started in the late 1930s and stayed active until 1975. The legacy at Milestone began with EEG's Old Faithful Lass and Ch. Milestone Monarch, who in turn produced Ch. Milestone Grande Duke and Ch. Milestone Magnificent. Ch. Milestone Matriarch, the daughter of Magnificent, became the founda-

Ch. Afternod Yank of Rockaplenty was the first Gordon Setter to win the Sporting Group at Westminster. He was owned by Mrs. W. W. Clark.

tion of the Sun-Yak kennel owned by Donald and Celeste Sunderland of Washington State.

Other kennels that emerged in the 1940s were Thurston's or Thor's Hill (owned by Arelyn Thurston of New York), Halenfred (owned by Harold Sydney of Rhode Island), Windy Hill (owned by Jake and Dottie Poisker of Pennsylvania), Gordon Hill (owned by Muriel Clement of Connecticut), Afternod (owned by Vincent and Marion Wilcox of Connecticut) and Sangerfield (owned by Margaret Sanger). All of these breeders devoted decades of their lives to the Gordon Setter breed, sharing their dogs, improving the breed, contributing to the development of the dual-purpose Gordon and promoting the breed throughout the country. Dozens of kennels to follow would not exist without the selfless work of these breeders.

The decade of the 1950s is marked by two ironic events: the revival of field trials for the breed, emphasizing the working attributes of the Gordon; and the first evidence of hip dysplasia in the breed, the bane of working dogs in nearly every breed. Among the new faces of the 1950s were Donald and Carol Chevalier (Loch Adair kennels), Cal and Elsye Calvert (Denida kennels), Ridgely and Pat Reichardt (Blarney Stone Gordon kennels), Ken Lasher (MacGregor kennels) and Warren and Stephanie Malvick. Among the top winners and producers of the decade were Ch. Blakeen Talisman, Ch. Fast's Falcon of Windy Hill, Ch. Heslop's Burnvale Duchess and Heslop's Burnvale Janet.

The first half of the 1960s belonged to two "special" Sangerfield boys: Smokey and Jed, both champions whose campaigns changed the course of Gordons in the show ring. Now Gordons were winning the Sporting Group consistently! Beginning in the 1960s, breeders began "specialing" a dog (that is, showing it past its championship to stack up wins). Additionally, two Best in Show victories occurred in Canada: Am./Can. Ch. Gunbar's Flapper, owned by Bill and Marge Platt, and Am./Can. Ch. Ger-Don's Ambrose Hobkirk, CD. One of the top dogs of the decade was Ch. Legend of Gael, CD, owned by Cheever Porter and handled by Robert and Jane Forsyth, whose career stretched until 1972 with an amazing 17 Bests in Show, 7 Bests in Specialty Show and 78 Group Ones.

The 1970s brought forth new legends: Ch. Torrance of Ellicott, the sire of 50 champions, owned by Mrs. Elizabeth Clark and J. Freundel; Ch. MacNeal of Ellicott, owned by Kay Monaghan; Ch. Afternod Yank of Rockaplenty, the sire of 83 champions, owned by Mrs. Elizabeth Clark; Ch. Daron

Ch. Daron Rebel With A Cause, top Gordon Setter of 1975, 1976 and 1977, was bred and owned by Ron and Darleen Wedeman in Arizona.

Rebel with a Cause, the sire of 13 champions and winner of 24 BIS, owned by Wedeman and Grant; and Ch. Ben-Wen's Benjy McDee, the winner of 27 BIS and 20 BISS.

FIELD TRIAL GORDONS
The parents of Gordon Setter trials are George and Jane

Ch. Ben-Wen's Benjy McDee, handled by Ross Petruzzo for owners Marie Annello and Barry Pearlstein. Benjy was the top Gordon Setter in 1978, 1979 and 1980.

Ch. Gordon Hill Alabama Slammer won the Sporting Group at Westminster in 1985, and was owned by Cindy Fitzgerald, Susan DeSilver and John Bandes.

Penterman, whose best dog, some say, was Field Champion (FC) Shuriridge Hummingbird, born in 1956. They also are credited with the first Dual Champion (DC), Loch Ridge Saegryte's Tibby; Page's Shuriridge Liz, who

Ch. Buteo's Great Miami, handled by Cathy Prickett for owner Gerald Curtis. Miami was the top Gordon Setter in 1986.

became the second Field Champion; and Ebony Sultan, Tibby's littermate, who became the third Field Champion. The Shuriridge kennels were in New Jersey.

Willard and Marjorie Platt of the Gunbar kennels in Illinois strived toward "dual perfection," Gordons that excelled in the field and in the show ring. Their first Dual Champion was DC Gunbar Dare Devil, CD.

One of the earliest field trial proponents, Alec Laurence began his Rhythm kennels in 1926 in California and continued producing and loving Gordons until his death in 1981. Among his well-known dogs were Ch. Rippling Rhythm, Ch. Rural Rhythm and Ch. Ravenscroft Jean's Debutante.

A true Gordon legend took to the field in 1951 in Jack Page's Shurridge Liz, winner of over 100 placements in her 9-year career. She produced many top-flight Gordons, including FC Page's Flash MacBess and Ch. Page's Captain MacGregor. Another spectacular Gordon from Page's kennel was Page's Jake, who finished his Field Championship at the tender age of two. Mr. Page also finished Page's Andrew of Elmust, Page's Dinan Rogue and Page's Janie of Cascades.

Nathan Putchat's Chance's Gordons have made a name in the field and show worlds, with such big winners as DC Windy Hill's Lucky Chance; DC Chance's National Velvet, CD; DC Glascott's Scottish Majesty; Bonnie's Mac's Macgeowls, CD; DC MacGeowls MacDougal and DC Glenraven Autumn Smoke.

Sam and Katherine Christine of Hacasak kennels in Pennsylvania produced their first Dual Champion in 1973 with DC Gordon Hill Lillipop and their second followed two years later, DC Hacasak Jenka's Lowako, CD.

FC MacGeowl's Braird helped put Dr. Joel and Barbara Morris on the map, when she finished the title in October 1969 at two years and eight months of age, the youngest FC bitch ever. Among the Belmor Farm's long line of Field Champions are FC Belmor's Pretty Missy, FC Belmor's Knight, FC Belmor's Allspice Ginger, FC Belmor's Pretty Belle, Belmor's Pretty Mister and DC St. Andrew Gaelic Brogue, CD.

Norman and Sue Sorby trained their first Dual Champion in DC/AFC Springset Duncan MacDuff, whom they acquired from Alec Laurence, upon whose dogs this excellent field kennel established itself in the early 1960s. Springset kennels in California has produced numerous Field Champions over its many years of breeding and trialing.

Jack and Barbara Cooper of the Shadowmere kennels, also in

Ch. Brawridge TNT of Kris, top Gordon Setter for 1988, 1989 and 1990, was also number-one Sporting Dog in 1988. TNT was owned by Charles Mann and R. L. Christianson.

California, are credited with many field greats including FC/AFC Springset Lady Bug, CD; DC Shadowmere Ebony Shane, CD; and DC Shadowmere Scylla Savoy. The Coopers' dogs have been named Gun Dog of the Year by the parent club for many (often consecutive) years.

Ch. Bit O Gold Titan Treasure was among the Top 10 dogs of all breeds for 1996, 1997 and 1998, #1 Sporting dog in 1996, and won 86 all-breed BIS in that time period. He was co-owned by breeder Peggy Nowak with Judy Browne and Susan Lybrand.

GORDON SETTER

The Gordon is a sturdy, rugged dog with exceptional skills in the field as well as a natural beauty that has brought him into the dog-showing spotlight.

ARE YOU A GORDON PERSON?
It is said of the Gordon Setter that once you own one, you would have no other breed and would wish that everyone could enjoy the companionship of this gentle dog. Over the years most Gordons have typically been kept as personal hunting companions and family pets. While their methodical style of hunting and dark coloring make them unpopular with those who prefer the smaller, faster dog for competition, the Gordon today is still a smart, stylish bird dog and a beauty in the show ring who is very competitive in all-breed events.

Gordons are alert and lively dogs with pleasant dispositions who are exceedingly loyal to their families. They are devoted to all members of their household but tend to be a bit aloof with strangers. They will tolerate attention from other people but will seldom make advances of their own until they accept a newcomer as a friend.

If a Gordon had his way, he would probably remain a puppy for eternity. This is a slow-maturing breed that remains puppy-like well into its second year, often peaking physically as late as four to six years of age. Gordon pups are playful and energetic, and they need early obedience training to channel their activities in the right direction. They are very biddable and willing to please and do not respond well to heavy-handed training methods, but with proper techniques they can be well trained without spoiling their happy disposition. Highly intelligent dogs, they will be quick to spot a weakness in an owner and try to claim the upper hand. Gordon puppies should attend basic obedience classes as early as allowed to shape their behavior and teach them the rules of social etiquette.

Gordons of all ages need plenty of daily exercise with frequent daily on-leash walks. Even if your Gordon is never used for hunting, he still requires lots of exercise to maintain peak physical and mental condition. A fenced yard is essential because, like many other gundog breeds, Gordons are creatures of their hunting instincts and will follow their noses after what they perceive as game.

As a good-sized breed, Gordons do best in larger home environments, although they will adapt to most living situations as long as they enjoy close and loving relationships with their families. They do best as house dogs, living indoors as part of the family, and will not thrive if relegated to kennel life. Of course, they enjoy plenty of outdoor activity with their favorite people!

Because the Gordon is so loyal to his owner, if you desire to send your dog out for professional training for the field, it is important to select a trainer who is familiar with the breed and is willing to spend extra time training the dog as an individual. One reason the Gordon Setter is a fine personal gundog is because he requires a close personal relationship with his owner as well as whoever oversees his training.

Gordon Setters as a breed are generally good with children,

SHEDDING
The Gordon Setter sheds his coat differently than does a Golden Retriever or a German Shepherd, with the Gordon's coat turning brown at the ends and taking a long time to fall out. The dead hair is easily removed by plucking it out, with your thumb and forefinger.

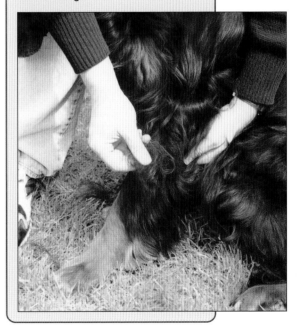

although they should be introduced to youngsters at an early age. Most tend to be protective of young family members. They will seldom growl or menace if children treat them harshly, preferring instead to simply withdraw from the offending child. That fact notwithstanding, all children should be taught that Gordons, indeed dogs of any breed, should always be treated with kindness and respect. Likewise, interactions between the dog and children should always be supervised.

Much has been written about the Gordon Setter's coat. Long,

> **BEAUTIFUL AND PRACTICAL**
> The profuse Gordon Setter coat is one of the breed's most appealing features. Considered to be the most rugged of all of the setter breeds, the Gordon has a long, dense coat that was developed to protect the dog when working in dense cover as well as in cold, rainy and otherwise inclement weather.

dense and heavily feathered, it is predominantly black with rich tan highlighting. Gordons usually do best in colder climates where the density of the coat is an asset in the grouse and woodcock woods. The long coat and heavy feathering do demand attention, but remember that the coat is designed to help the dog dig into heavy cover and protect him from brush and branches. A full weekly brushing and combing is essential to prevent mats and knots from forming in the coat; a daily once-over is recommended as well. The feet also require some attention. Uncut nails and untrimmed hair between the toes and footpads will cause discomfort as well as general breakdown of the feet.

HEALTH CONCERNS IN THE GORDON SETTER

HIP DYSPLASIA (HD)
Hip dysplasia simply means poor or abnormal development of the hip joint where the ball and socket do not fit together and function properly. It is common in most large breeds of dog and is considered to be an inherited disorder. A severe case of HD can render a working dog worthless in the field or other activities, and even a mild case can cause painful arthritis in the average house dog. While this condition is present in the Gordon Setter, it thankfully is less common than in many other large breeds.

While hip dysplasia is a largely inherited condition, research shows that environmental factors play a significant role in its development. Overfeeding and feeding a diet high in calories (primarily fat) during a large-breed puppy's rapid-growth stages are suspected to be contributing factors in the development of HD. Heavy-bodied and overweight puppies are more at risk than pups with lean conformation.

The Orthopedic Foundation for Animals (OFA) and other similar organizations offer x-ray testing and certification. Dogs 24 months of age and older should have their hips x-rayed and the x-rays sent to the OFA to determine if any degree of dysplasia is present. There are seven possible grades: Excellent, Good, Fair, Borderline, Mild, Moderate and Severe. Excellent, Good and Fair are considered normal and dogs with these gradings will receive an OFA number. The other four gradings do not warrant an OFA number, with the latter three indicating that the dog is affected by some level of dysplasia. Dogs that do not receive OFA numbers should not be used in breeding programs.

When visiting a litter, a potential owner should ask to see documentation of the litter's parents' hip clearances from OFA or another accredited organization; similar hip-testing programs are in

HEART-HEALTHY

In this modern age of ever-improving cardio-care, no doctor or scientist can dispute the advantages of owning a dog to lower a person's risk of heart disease. Studies have proven that petting a dog, walking a dog and grooming a dog all show positive results toward lowering your blood pressure. The simple routine of exercising your dog—going outside with the dog and walking, jogging or playing catch—is heart-healthy in and of itself. If you are normally less active than your physician thinks you should be, adopting a dog may be a smart option to improve your own quality of life as well as that of another creature.

place in countries around the world. Good breeders have all of their breeding stock tested and only breed from those dogs and bitches who have received appropriate clearances.

Do You Know about Hip Dysplasia?

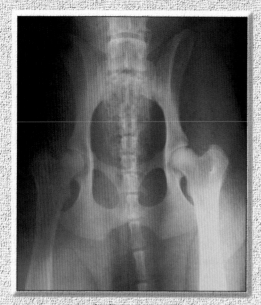

X-ray of a dog with "Good" hips.

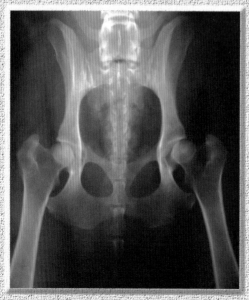

X-ray of a dog with "Moderate" dysplastic hips.

Hip dysplasia is a fairly common condition found in pure-bred dogs. When a dog has hip dysplasia, his hind leg has an incorrectly formed hip joint. By constant use of the hip joint, it becomes more and more loose, wears abnormally and may become arthritic.

Hip dysplasia can only be confirmed with an x-ray, but certain symptoms may indicate a problem. Your dog may have a hip dysplasia problem if he walks in a peculiar manner, hops instead of smoothly runs, uses his hind legs in unison (to keep the pressure off the weak joint), has trouble getting up from a prone position or always sits with both legs together on one side of his body.

As the dog matures, he may adapt well to life with a bad hip, but in a few years the arthritis develops and many dogs with hip dysplasia become crippled.

Hip dysplasia is considered an inherited disease and only can be diagnosed definitively by x-ray when the dog is two years old, although symptoms often appear earlier. Some experts claim that a special diet might help your puppy outgrow the bad hip, but the usual treatments are surgical. The removal of the pectineus muscle, the removal of the round part of the femur, reconstructing the pelvis and replacing the hip with an artificial one are all surgical interventions that are expensive, but they are usually very successful. Follow the advice of your veterinarian.

The purpose of such screening is to eliminate affected dogs from breeding programs, with the long-term goal of reducing the incidence of HD in the breeds involved. Gordon Setters who show marked evidence of hip dysplasia should never be bred. Anyone looking for a healthy Gordon Setter should make certain the sire and dam of any litter under consideration have their certificates of clearance.

A young dog moving with great enthusiasm. The gait should be free-moving and true, with plenty of drive behind, requiring sound skeletal structure.

BLOAT (GASTRIC DILATATION/VOLVULUS)

Bloat is a life-threatening condition that is most common in deep-chested breeds such as Gordon and Irish Setters, Bloodhounds, Great Danes and other similarly constructed breeds. It occurs when the stomach fills up rapidly with air and begins to twist, cutting off the blood supply. If not treated immediately, the dog will go into shock and die.

The development of bloat is sudden and unexplainable, although it typically involves feeding and exercise practices. The dog will become restless and his stomach will appear swollen or distended, and he will have difficulty breathing. The dog must receive veterinary attention at once in order to survive. The vet must relieve the pressure in the stomach and surgically return the stomach to its normal position.

Owners of deep-chested breeds must assume the responsibility for taking precautions to protect their dogs and reduce their risk of bloat. Preventive measures include:

- Feeding your dog several small meals rather than offering one large meal.
- Not exercising your dog for at least an hour before and two hours after eating.
- Making sure your dog is calm and not overly excited while he's eating. It has been shown that nervous or overly excited dogs are more prone to develop bloat.
- Adding a small portion of moist meat product to his dry food ration.

HYPOTHYROIDISM

Hypothyroidism is a condition in which the thyroid gland is under-active. One of the gland's major functions is regulating metabo-

Sparkling brown eyes on a young Gordon Setter, showing the proper intelligent and alert expression desirable in the breed.

lism, so reduced metabolism is one effect of hypothyroidism. Thyroid problems are seen in many breeds of dog, and hypothyroidism occurs with some frequency in the Gordon Setter. There is a genetic component to the condition, but it also can be influenced by environmental factors. Usually the onset occurs in the adult years.

Symptoms of hypothyroidism include overall decrease in energy, lack of interest in exercise, weight gain, skin and hair-loss problems, heat-seeking, behavioral changes and other abnormalities. Diagnosis begins by the vet's

examining your dog's medical and behavioral history and changes that have taken place. Next, blood tests will be done. The two tests that should be performed are the T4, which measures baseline levels of T4 hormone; and the TSH, which measures the level of thyroid stimulating hormone. The combination of these two usually provides an accurate diagnosis but there are other blood tests that can be done in combination with these to obtain more detail.

Hypothyroidism does not compromise a dog's lifespan; affected dogs can live normal, healthy lives with daily treatment and routine blood evaluations and check-ups as advised by the vet. Treatment involves daily dose of a synthetic hormone, which will keep symptoms at bay.

DELTA SOCIETY

The human-animal bond propels the work of the Delta Society, striving to improve the lives of people and animals. The Pet Partners Program proves that the lives of people and dogs are inextricably linked. The Pet Partners Program, a national registry, trains and screens volunteers for pet therapy in hospices, nursing homes, schools and rehabilitation centers. Dog-and-handler teams of Pet Partners volunteer in all 50 states, with nearly 7,000 teams making visits annually. About 900,000 patients, residents and students receive assistance each year. If you and your dog are interested in becoming Pet Partners, contact the Delta Society online at www.deltasociety.org.

What Is "Bloat" and How Do I Prevent it?

You likely have heard the term "bloat," which refers to gastric torsion (gastric dilatation/volvulus), a potentially fatal condition. As it is directly related to feeding and exercise practices, a brief explanation here is warranted. The term *dilatation* means that the dog's stomach is filled with air, while *volvulus* means that the stomach is twisted around on itself, blocking the entrance/exit points. Dilatation/volvulus is truly a deadly combination, although they also can occur independently of each other. An affected dog cannot digest food or pass gas, and blood cannot flow to the stomach, causing accumulation of toxins and gas along with great pain and rapidly occurring shock.

Many theories exist on what exactly causes bloat, but we do know that deep-chested breeds are more prone and that the risk doubles after seven years of age. Activities like eating a large meal, gulping water, strenuous exercise too close to mealtimes or a combination of these factors can contribute to bloat, though not every case is directly related to these more well-known causes. With that in mind, we can focus on incorporating simple daily preventives and knowing how to recognize the symptoms. In addition to the tips presented in this book, ask your vet about how to prevent and recognize bloat. An affected dog needs immediate veterinary attention, as death can result quickly. Signs include obvious restlessness/discomfort, crying in pain, drooling/excessive salivation, unproductive attempts to vomit or relieve himself, hardened abdomen, visibly bloated appearance and collapsing. Do not wait: get to the vet *right away* if you see any of these symptoms. The vet will confirm by x-ray if the stomach is bloated with air; if so, the dog must be treated *immediately*.

As varied as the causes of bloat are the tips for prevention, but some common preventive methods follow:
• Feed two or three small meals daily rather than one large one;
• Do not allow water before, after or with meals, but allow access to water at all other times;
• Never permit rapid eating or gulping of water;
• No exercise for the dog at least one hour before and two hours after meals;
• Feed high-quality food with adequate protein, adequate fiber content and not too much fat and carbohydrate;
• Explore herbal additives, enzymes or gas-reduction products (only under a vet's advice) to encourage a "friendly" environment in the dog's digestive system;
• Avoid foods and ingredients known to produce gas;
• Avoid stressful or overly excited situations for the dog, especially at mealtimes;
• Make dietary changes gradually, over a period of a few weeks;
• Do not feed dry food only;
• Although the role of genetics as a causative of bloat is not known, many breeders do not breed from previously affected dogs;
• Sometimes owners are advised to have gastroplexy (stomach stapling) performed on their dogs as a preventive measure.
Pay attention to your dog's behavior and any changes that could be symptomatic of bloat. Your dog's life depends on it!

GORDON SETTER

INTRODUCTION TO THE BREED STANDARD

The breed standard is the backbone of every breed of dog. This is the blueprint that dictates the characteristics of an ideal specimen of a given breed. It describes the physical appearance as well as the purpose of the breed, its temperament and its movement. The breed standard is generally based on the history of the breed and its original use or purpose. Of course, there is no such thing as the perfect dog, but by following the guidelines provided by the standard, breeders can continue to produce dogs that are true to the breed.

Every characteristic of the Gordon Setter relates to the Gordon as a total dog. Both form and function are mutually dependent if the Gordon is to look and perform at his very best. Most Gordons today perform only in the show ring, so it takes a conscientious breeder to keep the work-

The standard is the guide that breeders, judges and fanciers use to measure what is desirable in a Gordon Setter. This youngster, practicing a show stance, represents a breeder's hard work in trying to produce a Gordon that lives up to the standard.

ing traits of his dogs in mind when breeding expressly for the show ring. Attributes like proper head and amount and quality of coat tend to be emphasized over the dog's field abilities. Ideally breeders must keep the whole standard—the whole dog—in mind when planning a breeding, whether the ultimate goal is the field, the show ring or simply home and hearth.

THE AMERICAN KENNEL CLUB STANDARD FOR THE GORDON SETTER

General Appearance: The Gordon Setter is a good-sized, sturdily built, black and tan dog, well muscled, with plenty of bone and substance, but active, upstanding and stylish, appearing capable of doing a full day's work in the field. He has a strong, rather short back, with well sprung ribs and a short tail. The head is fairly heavy and finely chiseled. His bearing is intelligent, noble, and dignified, showing no signs of shyness or viciousness. Clear colors and straight or slightly waved coat are correct. He suggests strength and stamina rather than extreme speed. Symmetry and quality are most essential. A dog well balanced in all points is prefer-able to one with outstanding good qualities and defects. A smooth, free movement, with high head carriage, is typical.

Size, Proportion, Substance: *Size*—Shoulder height for males, 24 to 27 inches; females, 23 to 26 inches. Weight for males, 55 to 80 pounds; females, 45 to 70 pounds. Animals that appear to be over or under the prescribed weight limits are to be judged on the basis of conformation and condition. Extremely thin or fat dogs are discouraged on the basis that under- or overweight hampers the true working ability of the Gordon Setter. The weight-to-height ratio makes him heavier than other Setters. *Proportion*—The distance from the forechest to the back of

Head study showing pleasing type, proportion, substance and structure.

A mature dog groomed for show ring presentation. He exhibits good type, proportion and structure. The Gordon is the largest and most substantial of the setter breeds of the British Isles.

the thigh is approximately equal to the height from the ground to the withers. The Gordon Setter has plenty of bone and substance.

Head: Head deep, rather than broad, with plenty of brain room. *Eyes* of fair size, neither too deep-set nor too bulging, dark brown, bright and wise. The shape is oval rather than round. The lids are tight. *Ears* set low on the head approximately on line with the eyes, fairly large and thin, well folded and carried close to the head. *Skull* nicely rounded, good-sized, broadest between the ears. Below and above the eyes is lean and the cheeks as narrow as the leanness of the head allows. The head should have a clearly indicated stop. *Muzzle* fairly long and not pointed, either as seen from above or from the side. The flews are not pendulous. The muzzle is the same length as the skull from occiput to stop and the top of the muzzle is parallel to the line of the skull extended. *Nose* broad, with open nostrils and black in color. The lip line from the nose to the flews shows a sharp, well-defined, square contour. *Teeth* strong and white, meeting in front in a scissors bite, with the upper incisors slightly forward of the lower incisors. A level bite is not a fault. Pitted teeth from distemper or allied infections are not penalized.

nearly flat, with only a slight slope to the tailhead. *Tail* short and not reaching below the hocks, carried horizontal or nearly so, not docked, thick at the root and finishing in a fine point. The placement of the tail is important for correct carriage. When the angle of the tail bends too sharply at the first coccygeal bone, the tail will be carried too gaily or will

FAULTS IN PROFILE

Generally coarse and lacking type, coarse head, roman nose, ears set too high, low on leg, loaded upright shoulders, toes out in front, soft topline, low tail set, lack of angulation behind.

Muzzle underdeveloped, apple-headed, short neck, upright and heavy shoulders, wide in front, high in the rear, poor tail carriage, narrow rear that lacks angulation.

FAULTS IN PROFILE

Short coarse head, lacking stop with bumpy topskull, ewe neck, upright shoulders, toes out in front, long back, sloping topline, weak over-angulated rear.

Short muzzle, excessive dewlap, short thick neck, upright loaded shoulders, low on leg, long-backed, soft topline, steep in croup, weak pasterns, narrow rear, cowhocked.

Neck, Topline, Body: *Neck* long, lean, arched to the head and without throatiness. *Topline* moderately sloping. *Body* short from shoulder to hips. Chest deep and not too broad in front; the ribs well sprung, leaving plenty of lung room. The chest reaches to the elbows. A pronounced forechest is in evidence. Loins short and broad and not arched. Croup

With each litter, a good breeder tries to get closer to that ever-elusive ideal breed representative described in the standard.

deep heel cushions. Feet are not turned in or out.

Hindquarters: The hind legs from hip to hock are long, flat and muscular; from hock to heel, short and strong. The stifle and hock joints are well bent and not turned either in or out. When the dog is standing with the rear pastern perpendicular to the ground, the thighbone hangs downward parallel to an imaginary line drawn upward from the hock. Feet as in front.

droop. The tail placement is judged in relationship to the structure of the croup.

Forequarters: Shoulders fine at the points, and laying well back. The tops of the shoulder blades are close together. When viewed from behind, the neck appears to fit into the shoulders in smooth, flat lines that gradually widen from neck to shoulder. The angle formed by the shoulder blade and upper arm bone is approximately 90 degrees when the dog is standing so that the foreleg is perpendicular to the ground. Forelegs big-boned, straight and not bowed, with elbows free and not turned in or out. Pasterns are strong, short and nearly vertical with a slight spring. Dewclaws may be removed. Feet catlike in shape, formed by close-knit, well arched toes with plenty of hair between; with full toe pads and

Coat: Soft and shining, straight or slightly waved, but not curly, with long hair on ears, under stomach and on chest, on back of the fore and hind legs and on the tail. The feather which starts near the root of the tail is slightly waved or straight, having a triangular appearance, growing shorter uniformly toward the end.

Color and Markings: Black with tan markings, either of rich chestnut or mahogany color. Black pencilling is allowed on the toes. The borderline between black and tan colors is clearly defined. There are not any tan hairs mixed in the black. The tan markings are located as follows: (1) Two clear spots over the eyes and not over three-quarters of an inch in diameter; (2) On the sides of the muzzle. The tan does not reach to the top of the muzzle, but resembles a stripe around the end of the muzzle from one side to the other; (3) On the throat; (4) Two large clear spots on the chest; (5) On the inside of the hind legs showing down the front of the stifle and broadening out to the outside of the hind legs from the hock to the toes. It must not completely eliminate the black on the back of the hind legs; (6) On the forelegs from the carpus, or a little above, downward to the toes; (7) Around the vent; (8) A white spot on the chest is allowed, but the smaller the better. Predominantly tan, red or buff dogs which do not have the typical pattern of markings of a Gordon Setter are ineligible for showing and undesirable for breeding. Predominantly tan, red or buff dogs are ineligible for showing and undesirable for breeding.

Gait: A bold, strong, driving free-swinging gait. The head is carried up and the tail "flags" constantly while the dog is in motion. When viewed from the front the forefeet move up and down in straight lines so that the shoulder, elbow and pastern joints are approximately in line. When viewed from the rear the hock, stifle and hip joints are approximately in line. Thus the dog moves in a straight pattern forward without throwing the feet in or out. When viewed from the side the forefeet are seen to lift up and reach forward to

compensate for the driving hindquarters. The hindquarters reach well forward and stretch far back, enabling the stride to be long and the drive powerful. The overall appearance of the moving dog is one of smooth-flowing, well balanced rhythm, in which the action is pleasing to the eye, effortless, economical and harmonious.

Temperament: The Gordon Setter is alert, gay, interested and confident. He is fearless and willing, intelligent and capable. He is loyal and affectionate, and strong-minded enough to stand the rigors of training.

Disqualification: *Predominantly tan, red or buff dogs.*

Approved October 7, 2002
Effective November 27, 2002

SCALE OF POINTS:
To be used as a guide when judging the Gordon Setter:

Head and neck (include ears and eyes)	10
Body	15
Shoulders, forelegs, forefeet	10
Hind legs and feet	10
Tail	5
Coat	8
Color and markings	5
Temperament	10
Size, general appearance	15
Gait	12
Total	**100**

GORDON SETTER

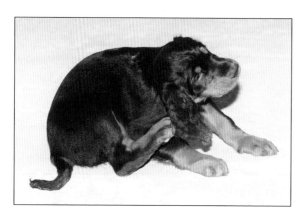

There's a sweet Gordon puppy out there just itching to find a place in your heart!

FINDING A GORDON SETTER PUPPY

The Gordon Setter is not an overly popular breed and thus puppies can be difficult to find. That in itself is a bonus for the breed, as it has not fallen into the hands of commercial breeders and suffered ill effects of careless overbreeding. However, it does complicate matters a bit for potential new owners, who will have to search a little harder for a breeder and available litter.

To get started, you should first decide on your intentions for the pup. Will he become a hunting partner or field-trial competitor? Do you plan to show him in the breed ring or train him for another competitive sport? Or will this Gordon live simply as a pet and family companion?

Once you have agreed on your goals for your new pup, you need to locate a responsible breeder who specializes in the particular area of your choice. Successful field trialers and ardent hunters breed only dogs from proven hunting stock that possess keen scenting and game-finding ability. The same is true of the serious show exhibitor who selects breeding stock for correct conformational properties. In all cases, the Gordon pups should be sound and healthy and have stable temperaments that are suitable for family life.

A good breeder should also be expected to ask you many ques-

COST OF OWNERSHIP
The purchase price of your puppy is merely the first expense in the typical dog budget. Quality dog food, veterinary care (sickness and health maintenance), dog supplies and grooming costs will add up to big bucks every year. Can you adequately afford to support a canine addition to the family?

tions about your intentions for his puppy and your ability to deal with the demands of owning a Gordon Setter. Quality breeders often have a waiting list for pups, and you may have to wait a year or more before a puppy is available. A good puppy is always worth the wait; after all, this Gordon will be with you for upward of a decade.

When launching your puppy search, prepare a list of questions in advance to determine if the breeder is responsible and has quality Gordon pups:

- Is the breeder a member of the Gordon Setter Club of America? The club is a trusted source for breeder referrals, as member breeders must uphold the club's code of ethics in their breeding programs.
- Are the sire and dam of the litter both registered with the American Kennel Club? Ask to see those registrations.
- Do both parents have hip clearances? Ask to see certification from the Orthopedic Foundation for Animals or another accredited organization proving that the sire and dam have tested free of hip dysplasia. The breeder should also show you the parents' clearances from the Canine Eye Registration Foundation (CERF), proving them free of hereditary eye disease.
- How often is the dam bred? A bitch should never be bred every

FINDING A QUALIFIED BREEDER

Before you begin your puppy search, ask for references from your veterinarian, other breeders and other Gordon owners to refer you to someone they believe is reputable. Responsible breeders usually raise only one or two breeds of dog. Avoid any breeder who has several different breeds or has several litters at the same time. Dedicated breeders are usually involved with a breed or other dog club. Many participate in some sport or activity related to their breed. Just as you want to be assured of the breeder's qualifications, the breeder wants to be assured that you will make a worthy owner. Expect the breeder to interview you, asking questions about your goals for the pup, your experience with dogs and what kind of home you will provide.

SIGNS OF A HEALTHY PUPPY

Healthy puppies are robust little fellows who are alert and active, sporting shiny coats and supple skin. They should not appear lethargic, bloated or pot-bellied, nor should they have flaky skin or runny or crusted eyes or noses. Their stools should be firm and well formed, with no evidence of blood or mucus.

season and should produce one litter a year at most.

- Are the breeder's premises clean, and is the litter's area also clean properly maintained and odor-free (within reason)?
- Are the other dogs on premises clean and well cared for? All the dogs should appear healthy and friendly with happy, stable temperaments.
- Does the pedigrees contain champions or field titles? Proven breeding stock is your only assurance that the pups will have the qualities you're looking for.
- Along with the breed club, is the breeder involved in other dog-related organizations and breed activities? Responsible breeders are usually involved in some aspect of the breed and the dog world as a whole.
- Have the pups been checked by a veterinarian? Have they had their first immunizations and are their health records up-to-date?

Be thorough in your discussions with the breeder. Evaluate his questions of you as well as his answers to those you ask. Selecting your Gordon means adding another member to your family, so making the right choice from the right source is important.

A COMMITTED NEW OWNER

By now you should understand what makes the Gordon Setter a most unique and special dog, one that may fit nicely into your family and lifestyle. If you have researched breeders, you should be able to recognize a knowledgeable and responsible Gordon Setter breeder who cares not only about his pups but also about what kind of owner you will be. If you have completed the final step in your new journey, you have found a litter, or possibly two, of quality Gordon Setter pups.

A visit with the puppies and their breeder should be an education in itself. Breed research, breeder selection and puppy visitation are very important aspects of finding the puppy of your dreams. Beyond that, these things also lay the foundation for a successful future with your pup. Puppy personalities within each

Brotherly love, Gordon Setter style! Littermates do everything together for at least their first eight weeks of life.

litter vary, from the shy and easygoing puppy to the one who is dominant and assertive, with most pups falling somewhere in between. By spending time with the puppies you will be able to recognize certain behaviors and what these behaviors indicate about each pup's temperament. Which type of pup will complement your family dynamics is best determined by observing the puppies in action within their "pack." Your breeder's expertise and recommendations are so valuable. Although you may fall in love with a bold and brassy male, the breeder may suggest that another pup would be best for you. The breeder's experience in rearing Gordon Setter pups and matching their temperaments with appropriate humans offers the

SELECTING FROM THE LITTER

Before you visit a litter of puppies, promise yourself that you won't fall for the first pretty face you see! Decide on your goals for your puppy—show prospect, hunting dog, obedience competitor, family companion—and then look for a puppy who displays the appropriate qualities. In most litters, there is an alpha pup (the bossy puppy), and occasionally a shy fellow who is less confident, with the rest of the litter falling somewhere in the middle. "Middle-of-the-roaders" are safe bets for most families and novice competitors.

GETTING ACQUAINTED

When visiting a litter, ask the breeder for suggestions on how best to interact with the puppies. If possible, get right into the middle of the pack and sit down with them. Observe which pups climb into your lap and which ones shy away. Toss a toy for them to chase and bring back to you. It's easy to fall in love with the puppy who picks you, but keep your future objectives in mind before you make your final decision.

survival—food, water, shelter and protection—he needs much, much more. The new pup needs love, nurturing and a proper canine education to mold him into a responsible, well-behaved canine citizen. Your Gordon Setter's health and good manners will need consistent monitoring and regular "tune-ups," so your job as a responsible dog owner will be ongoing throughout every stage of his life. If you are not prepared to accept these responsibilities and commit to them for at least the next decade, likely longer, then you are not prepared to own a dog of any breed.

Although the responsibilities of owning a dog may at times tax your patience, the joy of living with your Gordon Setter far outweighs the workload, and a well-mannered adult dog is worth your time and effort. Before your very eyes, your new charge will grow up to be your most loyal friend, devoted to you unconditionally.

YOUR GORDON SETTER SHOPPING LIST

Just as expectant parents prepare a nursery for their baby, so should you ready your home for the arrival of your Gordon Setter pup. If you have the necessary puppy supplies purchased and in place before he comes home, it will ease the puppy's transition from the warmth and familiarity of his mom and littermates to the brand-

best assurance that your pup will meet your needs and expectations. The type of puppy that you select is just as important as your decision that the Gordon Setter is the breed for you.

The decision to live with a Gordon Setter is a serious commitment and not one to be taken lightly. This puppy is a living sentient being that will be dependent on you for basic survival for his entire life. Beyond the basics of

THE DOG CRATE

If you think that crates are tools of punishment and confinement for when a dog has misbehaved, think again. Most breeders and almost all trainers recommend a crate as the preferred house-training aid as well as for all-around puppy training and safety. Because dogs are natural den creatures that prefer cave-like environments, the benefits of crate use are many. The crate provides the puppy with his very own "safe house," a cozy place to sleep, take a break or seek comfort with a favorite toy; a travel aid to house your dog when on the road, at motels or at the vet's office; a training aid to help teach your puppy proper toileting habits; a place of solitude when non-dog people happen to drop by and don't want a lively puppy—or even a well-behaved adult dog—saying hello or begging for their attention.

Crates come in several types, although the wire crate and the

The three most common crate types: wire on the left, mesh on the right and fiberglass on top.

new environment of his new home and human family. You will be too busy to stock up and prepare your house after your pup comes home, that's for sure! Imagine how a pup must feel upon being transported to a strange new place. It's up to you to comfort him and to let your little pup know that he is going to be happy with you!

FOOD AND WATER BOWLS

Your puppy will need separate bowls for his food and water. Stainless steel pans are generally preferred over plastic bowls since they sterilize better and pups are less inclined to chew on the metal. Heavy-duty ceramic bowls are popular, but consider how often you will have to pick up those heavy bowls! Buy adult-sized pans, as your puppy will grow into them quickly.

Gordon Setter puppies are playful, full of fun and, of course, adorable!

fiberglass airline-type crate are the most popular. Both are safe and your puppy will adjust to either one, so the choice is up to you. The wire crates offer better visibility for the pup as well as better ventilation. Many of the wire crates easily fold down into suitcase-sized carriers. The fiberglass crates, similar to those used by the airlines for animal transport, are sturdier and more den-like. However, the fiberglass crates do not fold and are less ventilated than wire crates, which can be problematic in hot weather. Some of the newer crates are made of heavy plastic mesh; they are very lightweight and fold up into slim-line suitcases. However, a mesh crate might not be suitable for a pup with manic chewing habits or a large adult like the Gordon.

Don't bother with a puppy-sized crate. Although your Gordon Setter will be a wee fellow when

A crate-trained dog will welcome the retreat of his own special space indoors or out, wherever you may go.

you bring him home, he will grow up in the blink of an eye and your puppy crate will be useless. Purchase a crate that will accommodate an adult Gordon Setter. He can stand up to 27 inches at the shoulder when full grown, so a crate measuring about 48 inches long by 30 inches wide by 36 inches high should fit him nicely.

BEDDING AND CRATE PADS
Your puppy will enjoy some type of soft bedding in his "room" (the crate), something he can snuggle into to feel cozy and secure. Old towels or blankets are good choices for a young pup, since he may (and probably will) have a toileting accident or two in the crate or decide to chew on the bedding material. Once he is fully

CRATE EXPECTATIONS

To make the crate more inviting to your puppy, you can offer his first meal or two inside the crate, always keeping the crate door open so that he does not feel confined. Keep a favorite toy or two in the crate for him to play with while inside. You can also cover the crate at night with a lightweight sheet to make it more den-like and remove the stimuli of household activity. Never put him into his crate as punishment or as you are scolding him, since he will then associate his crate with negative situations and avoid going there.

trained and out of the early chewing stage, you can replace the puppy bedding with a permanent crate pad if you prefer. Crate pads and other dog beds run the gamut from inexpensive to high-end doggie-designer styles, but don't splurge on the good stuff until you are sure that your puppy is reliable and won't tear it up or make a mess on it.

Puppy Toys

Just as infants and older children require objects to stimulate their minds and bodies, puppies need toys to entertain their curious brains, wiggly paws and achy teeth. A fun array of safe doggie toys will help satisfy your puppy's chewing instincts and distract him from gnawing on the

A Gordon puppy may start out small, but he represents a huge responsibility and longtime commitment for his new owners.

leg of your antique chair or your new leather sofa. Most puppy toys are cute and look as if they would be a lot of fun, but not all are necessarily safe or good for your puppy, so use caution when you go puppy-toy shopping.

Gordon Setter puppies are fairly aggressive chewers, so only the sturdiest toys should be offered to them. The best "chewcifiers" are nylon and hard rubber bones, which are safe to gnaw on and come in sizes appropriate for all age groups and breeds. Be especially careful of natural bones, which can splinter or develop dangerous sharp edges; pups can easily swallow or choke on those bone splinters. Veterinarians often tell of surgical nightmares involving bits of splintered bone, because in addition to the danger of choking, the sharp pieces can damage the intestinal tract.

Similarly, rawhide chews, while a favorite of most dogs and puppies, can be equally danger-

---

TEETHING TIME

All puppies chew. It's normal canine behavior. Chewing just plain feels good to a puppy, especially during the three- to five-month teething period when the adult teeth are breaking through the gums. Rather than attempting to eliminate such a strong natural chewing instinct, you will be more successful if you redirect it and teach your puppy what he may or may not chew. Correct inappropriate chewing with a sharp "No!" and offer him a chew toy, praising him when he takes it. Don't become discouraged. Chewing usually decreases after the adult teeth have come in.

ous. Pieces of rawhide are easily swallowed after they get soft and gummy from chewing, and dogs have been known to choke on large pieces of ingested rawhide. Rawhide chews should be offered only when you can supervise the puppy.

Soft woolly toys are special puppy favorites. They come in a wide variety of cute shapes and sizes; some look like little stuffed animals. Puppies love to shake them up and toss them about, or simply carry them around. Be careful of fuzzy toys that have button eyes or noses that your pup could chew off and swallow, and make sure that he does not disembowel a squeaky toy to remove the squeaker! Braided rope toys are similar in that they

are fun to chew and toss around, but they shred easily and the strings are easy to swallow. The strings are not digestible and, if the puppy doesn't pass them in his stool, he could end up at the vet's office. As with rawhides, your puppy should be closely monitored with rope toys.

If you believe that your pup has ingested a piece of one of his toys, check his stools for the next couple of days to see if he passes the item when he defecates. At the same time, also watch for signs of intestinal distress. A call to your veterinarian might be in order to get his advice and be on the safe side.

An all-time favorite toy for puppies (young and old!) is the empty gallon milk jug. Hard plas-

If not given proper chew toys and supervision, you can bet that puppies will have no problem finding something to sink their teeth into.

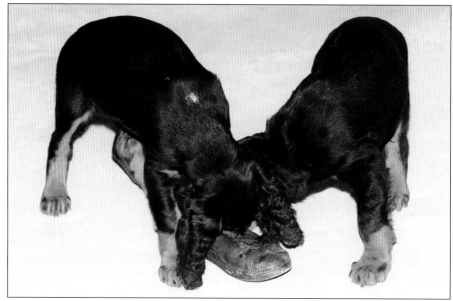

tic juice containers—46 ounces or more—are also excellent. Such containers make lots of noise when they are batted about, and puppies go crazy with delight as they play with them. However, they don't often last very long, so be sure to remove and replace them when they get chewed up.

A word of caution about homemade toys: be careful with your choices of non-traditional play objects. Never use old shoes or socks, since a puppy cannot distinguish between the old ones on which he's allowed to chew and the new ones in your closet that are strictly off limits. That principle applies to anything that resembles something that you don't want your puppy to chew.

COLLARS

A lightweight nylon collar is the best choice for a very young pup. Quick-click and buckle collars are easy to put on and remove, and they can be adjusted as the puppy grows. Introduce him to his collar as soon as he comes home to get him accustomed to wearing it. He'll get used to it quickly and won't mind a bit. Make sure that it is snug enough that it won't slip off, yet loose enough to be comfortable for the pup. You should be able to slip two fingers between the collar and his neck. Check the collar often, as puppies grow in spurts, and his collar can become too tight almost overnight.

TOYS 'R SAFE

The vast array of tantalizing puppy toys is staggering. Stroll through any pet shop or pet-supply outlet and you will see that the choices can be overwhelming. However, not all dog toys are safe or sensible. Most very young puppies enjoy soft woolly toys that they can snuggle with and carry around. (You know they have outgrown them when they shred them up!) Avoid toys that have buttons, tabs or other enhancements that can be chewed off and swallowed. Soft toys that squeak are fun, but make sure your puppy does not disembowel the toy and remove (and swallow) the squeaker. Toys that rattle or make noise can excite a puppy, but they present the same danger as the squeaky kind and so require supervision. Hard rubber toys that bounce can also entertain a pup, but make sure that the toy is too big for your pup to swallow.

Gordon Setters, like all gundogs, are orally fixated. Retrieving games keep your Gordon active and safely occupied.

There are various types of training collars, but these should not be used on young puppies.

Leashes

A 6-foot nylon lead is an excellent choice for a young puppy. It is lightweight and not as tempting to chew as a leather lead. You can switch to a 6-foot leather lead after your pup has grown and is used to walking politely on a lead. For initial puppy walks and house-training purposes, you should invest in a shorter lead so that you have more control over the puppy. At first, you don't want him wandering too far away from you, and when taking him out for toileting you will want to keep him in the specific area chosen for his potty spot.

Once the puppy is heel-trained with a traditional leash, you can consider purchasing a retractable lead. A retractable lead is excellent for walking adult dogs that are already leash-wise. This type of lead allows the dog to roam farther away from you and explore a wider area when out walking, and also retracts when you need to keep him close to you. Retractable leads come in different sizes and strengths based on dogs' weight, so be sure to purchase the strongest one for your Gordon.

HOME SAFETY FOR YOUR PUPPY

The importance of puppy-proofing cannot be overstated. In addition to making your house comfortable for your Gordon Setter's arrival, you also must make sure that your house is safe for your puppy

KEEP OUT OF REACH

Most dogs don't browse around your medicine cabinet, but accidents do happen! The drug acetaminophen, the active ingredient in some popular over-the-counter pain relievers, can be deadly to dogs and cats if ingested in large quantities. Acetaminophen toxicity, caused by the dog's swallowing 15 to 20 tablets, can be manifested in abdominal pains within a day or two of ingestion, as well as liver damage. If you suspect your dog has swiped a bottle of medication, get the dog to the vet immediately so that the vet can induce vomiting and cleanse the dog's stomach.

A Dog-Safe Home

The dog-safety police are taking you on a house tour. Let's go room by room and see how safe your own home is for your Gordon Setter. The following items are doggy dangers, so either they must be removed or the dog should be monitored or not have access to these areas.

LIVING ROOM
- house plants (some varieties are poisonous)
- fireplace or wood-burning stove
- paint on the walls (lead-based paint is toxic)
- lead drapery weights (toxic lead)
- lamps and electrical cords
- carpet cleaners or deodorizers

OUTDOOR
- swimming pool
- pesticides
- toxic plants
- lawn fertilizers

BATHROOM
- blue water in the toilet bowl
- medicine cabinet (filled with potentially deadly bottles)
- soap bars, bleach, drain cleaners, etc.
- tampons

KITCHEN
- household cleaners in the kitchen cabinets
- glass jars and canisters
- sharp objects (like kitchen knives, scissors and forks)
- garbage can (with remnants of good-smelling but dangerous things like onions, potato skins, apple or pear cores, peach pits, coffee beans, etc.)
- leftovers (some "people foods" are toxic to dogs)

GARAGE
- antifreeze
- fertilizers (including rose foods)
- pesticides and rodenticides
- pool supplies (chlorine and other chemicals)
- oil and gasoline in containers
- sharp objects, electrical cords and power tools

Until they are old enough to venture outside their quarters, the young litter does everything in the whelping box. The breeder works constantly to keep the pups' area clean and dry.

before you bring him home. There are countless hazards in the owner's personal living environment that a pup can sniff, chew, swallow or destroy. Many are obvious; others are not. Do a thorough advance house check to remove or rearrange those things that could hurt your puppy, keeping any potentially dangerous items out of areas to which he will have access.

Electrical cords are especially dangerous, since puppies view them as irresistible chew toys. Unplug and remove all exposed cords or fasten them beneath a baseboard where the puppy cannot reach them. Veterinarians and firefighters can tell you horror stories about electrical burns and house fires that resulted from puppy-chewed electrical cords. Consider this a most serious precaution for your puppy and the rest of your family.

Scout your home for tiny objects that might be seen at a pup's eye level. Keep medication bottles and cleaning supplies well out of reach, and do the same with waste baskets and other trash containers. It goes without saying that you should not use rodent poison or other toxic chemicals in any puppy area and that you must keep such containers safely locked up. You will be amazed at how many places a curious puppy can discover!

Once your house has cleared inspection, check your yard. A sturdy fence, well embedded into the ground, will give your dog a safe place to play and potty. Gordon Setters are large and athletic dogs, so a at least a 6-foot-high fence will be necessary to contain an agile youngster or adult. Check the fence periodically for necessary repairs. If there is a weak link or space to squeeze through, you can be sure that a

CONFINEMENT

It is wise to keep your puppy confined to a small "puppy-proofed" area of the house for his first few weeks at home. Gate or block off a space near the door that he will use for outdoor potty trips. Expandable baby gates are useful to create puppy's designated area. If he is allowed to roam through the entire house or even only several rooms, it will be more difficult to house-train him.

determined Gordon Setter will discover it.

The garage and shed can be hazardous places for a pup, as things like fertilizers, chemicals and tools are usually kept there. It's best to keep these areas off limits to the pup. Antifreeze is especially dangerous to dogs, as they find the taste appealing and it takes only a few licks from the driveway to kill a dog, puppy or adult, small breed or large.

VISITING THE VETERINARIAN

A good veterinarian is your Gordon Setter puppy's best health-insurance policy. If you do not already have a vet, ask friends and experienced dog people in your area for recommendations so that you can select a vet before you bring your Gordon Setter puppy home. Also arrange for your puppy's first veterinary examination beforehand, since many vets do not have appointments available immediately, and your puppy should visit the vet within a day or so of coming home.

It's important to make sure that your puppy's first visit to the vet is a pleasant and positive one. The vet should take great care to befriend the pup and handle him gently to make their first meeting a positive experience. The vet will give the pup a thorough physical examination and set up a schedule for vaccinations and other necessary wellness visits. Be sure to

TOXIC PLANTS
Plants are natural doggie magnets, but many can be harmful, even fatal, if ingested by a puppy or adult dog. Scout your yard and home interior and remove any plants, bushes or flowers that could be even mildly dangerous. It could save your dog's life. You can obtain a complete list of toxic plants from your veterinarian, at the public library or by looking online.

show your vet any health and inoculation records, which you should have received from your breeder. Your vet is a great source of canine health information, so be sure to ask questions and take notes. Creating a health journal for your puppy will make a handy reference for his wellness and any future health problems that may arise.

MEETING THE FAMILY

Your Gordon Setter's homecoming is an exciting time for all members of the family, and it's

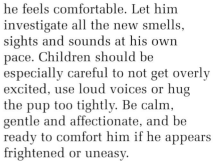

THE FAMILY FELINE

A resident cat has feline squatter's rights. The cat will treat the newcomer (your puppy) as she sees fit, regardless of what you do or say. So it's best to let the two of them work things out on their own terms. Cats have a height advantage and will generally leap to higher ground to avoid direct contact with a rambunctious pup. Some will hiss and boldly swat at a pup who passes by or tries to reach the cat. Keep the puppy under control in the presence of the cat and they will eventually become accustomed to each other.

Here's a hint: move the cat's litter box where the puppy can't get into it! It's best to do so well before the pup comes home so the cat is used to the new location.

he feels comfortable. Let him investigate all the new smells, sights and sounds at his own pace. Children should be especially careful to not get overly excited, use loud voices or hug the pup too tightly. Be calm, gentle and affectionate, and be ready to comfort him if he appears frightened or uneasy.

Be sure to show your puppy his new crate during this first day home. Toss a treat or two inside the crate; if he associates the crate with food, he will associate the crate with good things. If he is comfortable with the crate, you can offer him his first meal inside it. Leave the door ajar so he can wander in and out as he chooses.

FIRST NIGHT IN HIS NEW HOME

So much has happened in your Gordon Setter puppy's first day away from the breeder. He's had his first car ride to his new home. He's met his new human family and perhaps the other family pets. He has explored his new house and yard, at least those places where he is to be allowed during his first weeks at home. He may have visited his new veterinarian. He has eaten his first meal or two away from his dam and litter-mates. Surely that's enough to tire out an eight-week-old Gordon Setter pup...or so you hope!

It's bedtime. During the day, the pup investigated his crate,

only natural that everyone will be eager to meet him, pet him and play with him. However, for the puppy's sake, it's best to make these initial family meetings as uneventful as possible so that the pup is not overwhelmed with too much too soon. Remember, he has just left his dam and his littermates and is away from the breeder's home for the first time. Despite his fuzzy wagging tail, he is still apprehensive and wondering where he is and who all these strange humans are. It's best to let him explore on his own and meet the family members as

which is his new den and sleeping space, so it is not entirely strange to him. Line the crate with a soft towel or blanket that he can snuggle into and gently place him into the crate for the night. Some breeders send home a piece of bedding from where the pup slept with his littermates, and those familiar scents are a great comfort for the puppy on his first night without his siblings.

He will probably whine or cry. The puppy is objecting to the confinement and the fact that he is alone for the first time. This can be a stressful time for you as well as for the pup. It's important that you remain strong and don't let the puppy out of his crate to comfort him. He will fall asleep eventually. If you release him, the puppy will learn that crying means "out" and will continue

PUPPY PARASITES

Parasites are nasty little critters that live in or on your dog or puppy. Most puppies are born with ascarid roundworms, which are acquired from dormant ascarids residing in the dam. Other parasites can be acquired through contact with infected fecal matter. Take a stool sample to your vet for testing. He will prescribe a safe wormer to treat any parasites found in your puppy's stool. Always have a fecal test performed at your puppy's annual veterinary exam.

that habit. You are laying the groundwork for future habits. Some breeders find that soft music can soothe a crying pup and help him get to sleep.

SOCIALIZING YOUR PUPPY

The first 20 weeks of your Gordon Setter puppy's life are the most important of his entire lifetime. A properly socialized puppy will grow up to be a confident and stable adult who will be a pleasure to live with and a welcome addition to the neighborhood.

The importance of socialization cannot be overemphasized. Research on canine behavior has proven that puppies who are not exposed to new sights, sounds, people and animals during their first 20 weeks of life will grow up to be timid and fearful, even

The breeder starts the pup out on solid foods and should provide you with detailed feeding instructions for your pup as he grows.

aggressive, and unable to flourish outside of their familiar home environment.

Socializing your puppy is not difficult and, in fact, will be a fun time for you both. Lead training goes hand in hand with socialization, so your puppy will be learning how to walk on a lead at the same time that he's meeting the neighborhood. Because the Gordon Setter is such a terrific breed, everyone will enjoy meeting "the new kid on the block." Take him for short walks, to the park and to other dog-friendly places where he will encounter new people, especially children. Puppies automatically recognize children as "little people" and are drawn to play with them. Just make sure that you supervise these meetings and that the children do not get too rough or encourage him to play too hard. An overzealous pup can often nip too hard, frightening the child and in turn making the puppy overly excited. A bad experience in puppyhood can impact a dog for

life, so a pup that has a negative experience with a child may grow up to be shy or even aggressive around children.

Take your puppy along on your daily errands. Puppies are natural "people magnets," and most people who see your pup will want to pet him. All of these encounters will help to mold him into a confident adult dog. Likewise, you will soon feel like a confident, responsible dog owner, rightly proud of your mannerly Gordon Setter.

Be especially careful of your puppy's encounters and experiences during the eight-to-ten-week-old period, which is also called the "fear period." This is a serious imprinting period, and all contact during this time should be gentle and positive. A frightening or negative event could leave a permanent impression that could affect his future behavior if a similar situation arises.

Also make sure that your puppy has received his first and second rounds of vaccinations before you expose him to other dogs or bring him to places that other dogs may frequent. Avoid dog parks and other strange-dog areas until your vet assures you that your puppy is fully immunized and resistant to the diseases that can be passed between canines. Discuss safe socialization with your breeder and vet, as some recommend socializing the

ESTABLISH A ROUTINE

Routine is very important to a puppy's learning environment. To facilitate house-training, use the same exit/entrance door for potty trips and always take the puppy to the same place in the yard. The same principle of consistency applies to all other aspects of puppy training.

puppy even before he has received all of his inoculations, depending on how outgoing the breed or puppy may be.

LEADER OF THE PUPPY'S PACK

Like other canines, your puppy needs an authority figure, some-one he can look up to and regard as the leader of his "pack." His first pack leader was his dam, who taught him to be polite and not chew too hard on her ears or nip at her muzzle. He learned those same lessons from his litter-mates. If he played too rough, they cried in pain and stopped the game, which sent an important message to the rowdy puppy.

As puppies play together, they are also struggling to determine who will be the boss. Being pack

animals, dogs need someone to be in charge. If a litter of puppies remained together beyond puppy-hood, one of the pups would emerge as the strongest one, the one who calls the shots.

Once your puppy leaves the pack, he will look intuitively for a new leader. If he does not recog-nize you as that leader, he will try to assume that position for himself. Of course, it is hard to imagine your adorable Gordon Setter puppy trying to be in charge when he is so small and seemingly help-less. You must remember that these are natural canine instincts. Do not cave in and allow your pup to get the upper "paw"!

Just as socialization is so important during these first 20 weeks, so too is your puppy's early education. He was born without any bad habits. He does not know

Along with love and care, your puppy needs guidance to feel secure. Consistency and positive reinforcement are keys to teaching your pup.

DIGGING OUT

Some dogs love to dig. Others wouldn't think of it. Digging is considered "self-rewarding behavior" because it's fun! Of all the digging solutions offered by the experts, most are only marginally successful and none are guaranteed to work. The best cure is prevention, which means removing the dog from the offending site when he digs as well as distracting him when you catch him digging so that he turns his attentions elsewhere. That means that you have to supervise your dog's yard time. An unsupervised digger can create havoc with your landscaping or, worse, run away!

what is good or bad behavior. If he does things like nipping and digging, it's because he is having fun and doesn't know that humans consider these things as "bad." It's your job to teach him proper puppy manners, and this is the best time to accomplish that—before he has developed bad habits, since it is much more difficult to "unlearn" or correct unacceptable learned behavior than to teach good behavior from the start.

Make sure that all members of the family understand the importance of being consistent when training their new puppy. If you tell the puppy to stay off the sofa and your daughter allows him to cuddle on the couch to watch her favorite television show, your pup will be confused about what he is and is not allowed to do. Have a family conference before your pup comes home so that everyone understands the basic principles of puppy training and the rules you have set forth for the pup, and agrees to follow them.

The old saying that "an ounce of prevention is worth a pound of cure" is especially true when it comes to puppies. It is much easier to prevent inappropriate behavior than it is to change it. It's also easier and less stressful for the pup, since it will keep discipline to a minimum and create a more positive learning environment for him. That, in turn, will also be easier on you!

SOLVING PUPPY PROBLEMS

CHEWING AND NIPPING

Nipping at fingers and toes is normal puppy behavior. Chewing is also the way that puppies investigate their surroundings. However, you will have to teach your puppy that chewing anything other than his toys is not acceptable. That won't happen overnight and at times puppy teeth will test your patience. However, if you allow nipping and chewing to continue, just think about the damage that a mature Gordon Setter can do with a full set of adult teeth.

SWEETS THAT KILL

Antifreeze would be every dog's favorite topping for a chocolate sundae! However, antifreeze, just like chocolate, kills dogs. Ethylene glycol, found in antifreeze, causes acute renal failure in dogs and can be fatal. Dogs suffering from kidney failure expel little or no urine, act lethargically, may experience vomiting or diarrhea and may resist activity and drinking water. Just a single teaspoon of antifreeze is enough to kill a dog (depending on the size); even for large dogs it takes only a tablespoon or two! Like that irresistible chocolate, antifreeze is sweet-tasting and smells yummy. Keep them away from your dog!

Whenever your puppy nips your hand or fingers, cry out "Ouch!" in a loud voice, which should startle your puppy and stop him from nipping, even if only for a moment. Immediately distract him by offering a small treat or an appropriate toy for him to chew instead (which means having chew toys and puppy treats handy or in your pockets at all times). Praise him when he takes the toy and tell him what a good fellow he is. Praise is just as or even more important in puppy training as discipline and correction.

Puppies also tend to nip at children more often than adults, since they perceive little ones to be more vulnerable and more similar to their littermates. Teach your children appropriate responses to nipping behavior. If

they are unable to handle it themselves, you may have to intervene. Puppy nips can be quite painful and a child's frightened reaction will only encourage a puppy to nip harder, which is a natural canine response. As with all other puppy situations, interaction between your Gordon Setter puppy and children should be supervised.

Chewing on objects, not just family members' fingers and ankles, is also normal canine behavior that can be especially tedious (for the owner, not the pup) during the teething period when the puppy's adult teeth are coming in. At this stage, chewing just plain feels good. Furniture legs and cabinet corners are common puppy favorites. Shoes and other personal items also taste pretty good to a pup.

The best solution is, once again, prevention. If you value

Puppies are curious creatures, exploring with their paws and mouths. You must consider the safety of both your puppy and your belongings.

Bright and alert, this baby Gordon can't wait to meet the world!

something, keep it tucked away and out of reach. You can't hide your dining-room table in a closet, but you can try to deflect the chewing by applying a bitter product made just to deter dogs from chewing. Available in a spray or cream, this substance is vile-tasting, although safe for dogs, and most puppies will avoid the forbidden object after one tiny taste. You also can apply the product to your leather leash if the puppy tries to chew on his lead during leash-training sessions.

Keep a ready supply of safe chews handy to offer your Gordon Setter as a distraction when he starts to chew on something that's a "no-no." Remember, at this tender age, he does not yet know what is permitted or forbidden, so you have to be "on call" every minute he's awake and on the prowl.

You may lose a treasure or two during puppy's growing-up period, and the furniture could sustain a nasty nick or two. These can be trying times, so be prepared for those inevitable accidents and comfort yourself in knowing that this too shall pass.

Puppy Whining

Puppies often cry and whine, just as infants and little children do. It's their way of telling us that they are lonely or in need of attention. Your puppy will miss his littermates and will feel insecure when he is left alone. You may be out of the house or just in another room, but he will still feel alone. During these times, the puppy's crate should be his personal comfort station, a place all his own where he can feel safe and secure. Once he learns that being alone is okay and not something to be feared, he will settle down without crying or objecting. You might want to leave a radio on while he is crated, as the sound of human voices can be soothing and will give the impression that people are around.

Give your puppy a favorite cuddly toy or chew toy to entertain him whenever he is crated. You will both be happier: the puppy because he is safe in his den and you because he is quiet,

Forbidden items like dishrags and socks are puppy favorites as they are soft and feel good to a teething mouth.

safe and not getting into puppy escapades that can wreak havoc in your house or cause him danger.

To make sure that your puppy will always view his crate as a safe and cozy place, never, ever use the crate as punishment. That's the best way to turn the crate into a negative place that the pup will want to avoid. Sure, you can use the crate for your own peace of mind if your puppy is getting into trouble and needs some "time out." Just don't let him know that! Never scold the pup and immediately place him into the crate. Count to ten, give him a couple of hugs and maybe a treat, then scoot him into his crate.

It's also important not to make a big fuss when he is released from the crate. That will make getting out of the crate more appealing than being in the crate, which is just the opposite of what you are trying to achieve.

FOUR ON THE FLOOR

You must discourage your dog from jumping up to get attention or for any other reason. To do so, turn and walk away from the dog as he jumps up, not allowing him to get his paws on you. "Four on the floor" requires praise. Once the dog sits on command, prevent him from attempting to jump again by asking him to sit/stay before petting him. Back away if he breaks the sit.

"COUNTER SURFING"

What we like to call "counter surfing" usually starts to happen as soon as a puppy realizes that he is big enough to stand on his hind legs and investigate the good stuff on the kitchen counter or the coffee table. Once again, you have to be there to prevent it! As soon as you see your Gordon Setter even start to raise himself up, startle him with a sharp "No!" or "Aaahh, aaahh!" If he succeeds and manages to get one or both paws on the forbidden surface, give him a firm "Off" command as you place his feet back on the ground. As soon as he's back on all four paws, command him to sit and praise at once.

For surf prevention, make sure to keep any tempting treats or edibles out of reach, where your Gordon Setter can't see or smell them. It's the old rule of prevention yet again.

Take care when using a crate outdoors. Heat stroke is a common killer of dogs, so always be sure your dog has shade and water when outdoors.

PROPER CARE OF YOUR
GORDON SETTER

Adding a Gordon Setter to your household means adding a new family member who will need your care each and every day. When your Gordon Setter pup first comes home, you will start a routine with him so that, as he grows up, your dog will have a daily schedule just as you do. The aspects of your dog's daily care will likewise become regular parts of your day, so you'll both have a new schedule. Dogs learn by consistency and thrive on routine: regular times for meals, exercise, grooming and potty trips are just as important for your dog as they are to you! Your dog's schedule will depend much on your family's daily routine, but remember that you now have a new member of the family who is part of your day every day!

FEEDING

Feeding your dog the best diet is based on various factors, including age, activity level, overall condition and size of breed. When you visit the breeder, he will share with you his advice about the proper diet for your dog based on his experience with the breed and the foods with which he has had success. Likewise, your vet will be a helpful source of advice throughout the dog's life and will aid you in planning a diet for optimal health.

FEEDING THE PUPPY

Of course, your pup's very first food will be his dam's milk. There may be special situations in which pups fail to nurse, necessitating that the breeder hand-feed

---

NOT HUNGRY?

No dog in his right mind would turn down his dinner, would he? If you notice that your dog has lost interest in his food, there could be any number of causes. Dental problems are a common cause of appetite loss, one that is often overlooked. If your dog has a toothache, a loose tooth or sore gums from infection, chances are it doesn't feel so good to chew. Think about when you've had a toothache! If your dog does not approach the food bowl with his usual enthusiasm, look inside his mouth for signs of a problem. Whatever the cause, you'll want to consult your vet so that your chow hound can get back to his happy, hungry self as soon as possible.

them with a formula, but for the most part pups spend the first weeks of life nursing from their dam. The breeder weans the pups by gradually introducing solid foods and decreasing the milk meals. Pups may even start themselves off on the weaning process, albeit inadvertently, if they snatch bites from their mom's food bowl.

By the time the pups are ready for new homes, they are fully weaned and eating a good puppy food. As a new owner, you may be thinking, "Great! The breeder has taken care of the hard part." Not so fast.

A puppy's first year of life is the time when all or most of his growth and development takes place. This is a delicate time, and diet plays a huge role in proper skeletal and muscular formation. Improper diet and exercise habits can lead to damaging problems that will compromise the dog's health and movement for his entire life. That being said, new owners should not worry needlessly. With the myriad types of food formulated specifically for growing pups of different-sized breeds, dog-food manufacturers have taken much of the guesswork out of feeding your puppy well. Since growth-food formulas are designed to provide the nutrition that a growing puppy needs, it is unnecessary and, in fact, can prove harmful to add supplements to the diet. A good puppy formula

is designed to promote healthy, not rapid, growth. Further, research has shown that too much of certain vitamin supplements and minerals predispose a dog to skeletal problems. It's by no means a case of "if a little is good, a lot is better." At every stage of your dog's life, too much or too little in the way of nutrients can be harmful, which is why a manufactured complete food is the easiest way to know that your dog is getting what he needs.

Because of a young pup's small body and accordingly small digestive system, his daily portion

Your Gordon Setter's diet impacts his coat quality, temperament, energy level and overall health. Select the most suitable diet with the assistance of your breeder and/or vet.

Mother's milk
provides the
pups with the
best start in
life.

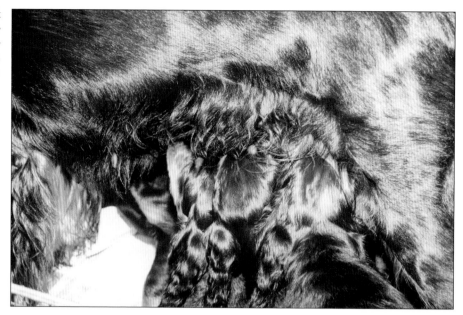

will be divided up into small meals throughout the day. This can mean starting off with three or more meals a day and decreasing the number of meals as the pup matures. For the adult Gordon Setter, dividing the day's food into two meals on a morning/evening schedule is healthier for the dog's digestion than one large daily portion.

Regarding the feeding schedule, feeding the pup at the same times and in the same place each day is important for both housebreaking purposes and establishing the dog's everyday routine. As for the amount to feed, growing puppies generally need proportionately more food per body weight than their adult counter-

parts, but a pup should never be allowed to gain excess weight. Dogs of all ages should be kept in proper body condition, but extra weight can strain a pup's developing frame, causing skeletal problems.

Watch your pup's weight as he grows and, if the recommended amounts seem to be too much or too little for your pup, consult the vet about appropriate dietary changes. Keep in mind that treats, although small, can quickly add up throughout the day, contributing unnecessary calories. Treats are fine when used prudently; opt for dog treats specially formulated to be healthy or for nutritious snacks like small pieces of cheese or cooked chicken.

FEEDING THE ADULT DOG

For the adult (meaning physically mature) dog, feeding properly is about maintenance, not growth. The Gordon Setter grows slowly and takes a few years to mature physically but he generally can be switched to an adult food around one year of age. Again, correct weight is a concern. Your dog should appear fit and should have an evident "waist." His ribs

SWITCHING FOODS

There are certain times in a dog's life when it becomes necessary to switch his food; for example, from puppy to adult food and then from adult to senior-dog food. Additionally, you may decide to feed your pup a different type of food from what he received from the breeder, and there may be "emergency" situations in which you can't find your dog's normal brand and have to offer something else temporarily. Anytime a change is made, for whatever reason, the switch must be done gradually. You don't want to upset the dog's stomach or end up with a picky eater who refuses to eat something new. A tried-and-true approach is, over the course of about a week, to mix a little of the new food in with the old, increasing the proportion of new to old as the days progress. At the end of the week, you'll be feeding his regular portions of the new food, and he will barely notice the change.

should not be protruding (a sign of being underweight), but they should be covered by only a slight layer of fat. Under normal circumstances, an adult dog can be maintained fairly easily with a high-quality nutritionally complete adult-formula food.

Factor treats into your dog's overall daily caloric intake, and avoid offering table scraps. Not only are some "people foods," including chocolate, nuts onions, grapes and raisins, toxic to dogs but feeding table scraps also encourages begging, fussiness and overeating. Overweight dogs are more prone to health problems. Research has even shown that obesity takes years off a dog's life. With that in mind, resist the urge to overfeed and over-treat. Don't make unnecessary additions to your dog's diet, whether with tidbits or with extra vitamins and minerals.

The breeder introduces solid food at the appropriate time; the pups will be fully weaned when they go to their new homes.

preventives related to exercise, feeding and water.

DIETS FOR THE AGING DOG

A good rule of thumb is that once a dog has reached 75% of his expected lifespan, he has reached "senior citizen" or geriatric status. Your Gordon Setter will be considered a senior at about 7

A complete and balanced dog food, fed in proper portions, makes it easy to provide good nutrition to your Gordon.

The amount of food needed for proper maintenance will vary depending on the individual dog's activity level, but you will be able to tell whether the daily portions are keeping him in good shape. With the wide variety of good complete foods available, choosing what to feed is largely a matter of personal preference. Just as with the puppy, the adult dog should have consistency in his mealtimes and feeding place. In addition to a consistent routine, regular mealtimes also allow the owner to see how much his dog is eating. If the dog seems never to be satisfied or, likewise, becomes uninterested in his food, the owner will know right away that something is wrong and can consult the vet. Scheduled mealtimes also allow owners to practice the important bloat

FEEDING AN ACTIVE DOG

The more a dog does, the more he needs to eat! Examples of dogs with higher nutrient requirements are dogs who are very active in training for or competing in sporting disciplines, and dogs that are used in a working capacity such as hunting or herding. They do not need supplementation to their regular food; rather, because they need larger amounts of all nutrients, they will need their maintenance food in larger portions. Also ask your vet about specially formulated "performance" diets for active dogs.

When feeding an active dog, it is essential to provide adequate periods of rest before and after eating to avoid stomach upset or the more serious gastric torsion, which can be fatal. Treats can be fed during rest periods as well to keep up the dog's energy in between meals, and plenty of water given. The dog needs time to settle down before and after any eating or drinking, so breaks should be factored into the training program or work routine.

years of age; based on his size and other factors, he has an average lifespan of about 10–12 years, although he can live longer. (The smallest breeds generally enjoy the longest lives and the largest breeds the shortest.)

What does aging have to do with your dog's diet? No, he won't get a discount at the local diner's early-bird special. Yes, he will require some dietary changes to accommodate the changes that come along with increased age. One change is that the older dog's dietary needs become more similar to that of a puppy. Specifically, dogs can metabolize more protein as youngsters and seniors than in the adult-maintenance stage. Discuss with your vet whether you need to switch to a higher-protein or senior-formulated food or whether your current adult-dog food contains sufficient nutrition for the senior.

Watching the dog's weight remains essential, even more so in the senior stage. Older dogs are already more vulnerable to illness, and obesity only contributes to their susceptibility to problems. As the older dog becomes less active and, thus, exercises less, his regular portions may cause him to gain weight. At this point, you may consider decreasing his daily food intake or switching to a reduced-calorie food. As with other changes, you should consult your vet for advice.

DON'T FORGET THE WATER!

Regardless of what type of food he eats, there's no doubt that your Gordon needs plenty of water. Fresh cold water, in a clean bowl, should be available to your dog. There are special circumstances, such as during puppy housebreaking, when you will want to moni-

DIET DON'TS

- Got milk? Don't give it to your dog! Dogs cannot tolerate large quantities of cows' milk, as they do not have the enzymes to digest lactose.
- You may have heard of dog owners who add raw eggs to their dogs' food for a shiny coat or to make the food more palatable, but consumption of raw eggs too often can cause a deficiency of the vitamin biotin.
- Avoid feeding table scraps, as they will upset the balance of the dog's complete food. Additionally, fatty or highly seasoned foods can cause upset canine stomachs.
- Do not offer raw meat to your dog. Raw meat can contain parasites; it also is high in fat.
- Vitamin A toxicity in dogs can be caused by too much raw liver, especially if the dog already gets enough vitamin A in his balanced diet, which should be the case.
- Bones like chicken, pork chop and other soft bones are not suitable, as they easily splinter.

moisten dry food with milk, but dogs do not have the enzymes necessary to digest the lactose in milk, which is much different from the milk that nursing puppies receive. Therefore stick with clean fresh water to quench your dog's thirst.

A word of caution concerning your deep-chested Gordon Setter's water intake: he should never be allowed to gulp water, especially at mealtimes. In fact, his water intake should be limited at mealtimes as a rule. He should be allowed water to cool down after exercise, but never allowed to gulp. These simple daily precautions can go a long way in protecting your dog from the dangerous and potentially fatal gastric torsion (bloat).

EXERCISE

All gundog breeds require more exercise than most other breeds, and the Gordon Setter, though not

While elevated bowls were once thought of as a bloat preventive, there is now much debate over whether raising the bowls helps or actually increases the risk.

tor your pup's water intake so that you will be able to predict when he will need to relieve himself, but water must be available to him nonetheless. Water is essential for hydration and proper body function just as it is in humans.

You will get to know how much your dog typically drinks in a day. Of course, in the heat or if exercising vigorously, he will be more thirsty and will drink more. However, if he begins to drink noticeably more water for no apparent reason, this could signal any of various problems, and you are advised to consult your vet.

Water is the best drink for dogs. Some owners are tempted to give milk from time to time or to

FEEDING IN HOT WEATHER

Even the most dedicated chow hound may have less of an appetite when the weather is hot or humid. If your dog leaves more of his food behind than usual, adjust his portions until the weather and his appetite return to normal. Never leave the uneaten portion in the bowl, hoping he will return to finish it, because higher temperatures encourage food spoilage and bacterial growth.

the most active of the hunting breeds, is no exception. A sedentary lifestyle is as harmful to a dog as it is to a person. The Gordon Setter, a large dog with fairly long legs, needs to be walked twice daily for considerable distances. He also needs free-running time as well to keep himself fit. This can be in your own fenced yard, an off-leash dog park or another securely enclosed area. If you live in an apartment or a house without a large fenced yard, you will have to commit to walking the dog for a few miles each day. For those who are more ambitious, you will find that your Gordon Setter also enjoys longer walks, an occasional hike, games of fetch or even a swim!

Bear in mind that an overweight dog should never be suddenly over-exercised; instead

Although a thirsty Gordon can drink water by the bucketful, it's never wise to allow your Gordon to gulp water.

he should be encouraged to increase exercise slowly. Not only is exercise essential to keep the dog's body fit, it is essential to his mental well-being. A bored dog will find something to do, which often manifests itself in some type of destructive behavior. In this sense, exercise is just as essential for the owner's mental well-being!

GROOMING

BRUSHING
The grooming tool of choice for your Gordon Setter is a natural bristle brush, which can be used for regular routine brushing. Brushing every other day is effective for removing dead hair and stimulating the dog's natural oils to add shine and a healthy look to the coat. In addition to keeping the Gordon's coat mat-free, regular

PUPPY STEPS
Puppies are brimming with activity and enthusiasm. It seems that they can play all day and night without tiring, but don't overdo your puppy's exercise regimen. Easy does it for the puppy's first six to nine months. Keep walks brief and don't let the puppy engage in stressful jumping games. The puppy frame is delicate, and too much exercise during those critical growing months can cause injury to his bone structure, ligaments and musculature. Save his first jog for his first birthday!

Plucking is a useful technique with a Gordon Setter. Simply grasp a few dead hairs (with brown ends) and gently pull them out in the direction the coat grows. Be gentle and this will not hurt the dog.

grooming sessions are also a good way to spend time with your dog.

The Gordon Setter coat sheds differently than those of the double-coated breeds. The dead hairs turn brown at the ends and take a while to fall out. The owner can assist in the shedding process by plucking to remove the dead hair from the coat. This is important so that the dead hair does not mat into the coat. "Plucking," a term usually used to describe the grooming of a terrier's coat, is accomplished by pulling out hairs from the root by grasping small clumps of hair between the thumb and forefinger. Care also should be taken when tending to the ears, which are well furnished and require some tidying to keep looking nice. For the working Gordon Setter who will spend time in wooded areas, the owner must tend to burrs and twigs that can become entangled in his dog's coat.

BATHING

In general, dogs need to be bathed only a few times a year, possibly more often if your dog gets into something messy or if he starts to smell like a dog. Show dogs are usually bathed before every show, which could be as frequent as weekly, although this depends on the owner. Bathing too frequently can have negative effects on the skin and coat, removing natural oils and causing dryness.

If you give your dog his first bath when he is young, he will become accustomed to the process. Wrestling a dog into the tub or chasing a freshly shampooed dog who has escaped from the bath will be no fun! Most dogs don't naturally enjoy their baths, but you at least want yours to cooperate with you.

Before bathing the dog, have the items you'll need close at hand. First, decide where you will bathe the dog. You should have a

Regular brushing and combing, along with an occasional bath, should keep the Gordon's coat healthy, silky and clean.

WATER SHORTAGE

No matter how well behaved your dog is, bathing is always a project! Nothing can substitute for a good warm bath, but owners do have the option of giving their dogs "dry" baths. Pet shops sell excellent products, in both powder and spray forms, designed for spot-cleaning your dog. These dry shampoos are convenient for touch-up jobs when you don't have the time to bathe your dog in the traditional way.

Muddy feet, messy behinds and smelly coats can be spot-cleaned and deodorized with a "wet-nap"-style cleaner. On those days when your dog insists on rolling in fresh goose droppings and there's no time for a bath, a spot bath can save the day. These pre-moistened wipes are also handy for other grooming needs like wiping faces, ears and eyes and freshening tails and behinds.

tub or basin with a non-slip surface. In warm weather, some like to use a portable pool in the yard, although you'll want to make sure your dog doesn't head for the nearest dirt pile following his bath! You will also need a hose or shower spray to wet the coat thoroughly, a shampoo formulated for dogs, absorbent towels and perhaps a blow dryer. Human shampoos are too harsh for dogs' coats and will dry them out.

Before wetting the dog, give him a brush-through to remove any dead hair, dirt and mats.

Use thinning shears on the outside of the ear to tidy up the appearance.

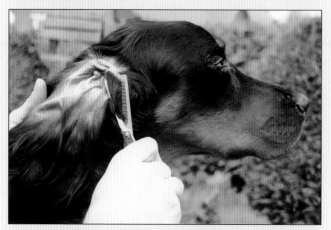

Thinning shears also can be used to minimize any "tufts" that grow around the ears.

Tidying the tail may be required to neaten up its outline and present an appealing silhouette.

SELECTING THE RIGHT BRUSHES AND COMBS

Will a rubber curry make my dog look slicker? Is a rake smaller than a pin brush? Do I choose nylon or natural bristles? Buying a dog brush can make the hairs on your head stand on end! Here's a quick once-over to educate you on the different types of brushes.

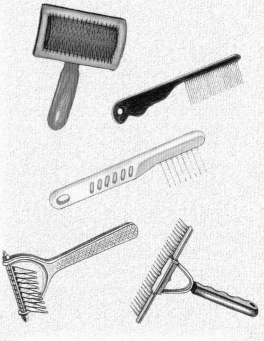

Slicker Brush: Fine metal prongs closely set on a curved base. Used to remove dead coat from the undercoat of medium- to long-coated breeds.

Pin Brush: Metal pins, often covered with rubber tips, set on an oval base. Used to remove shedding hair and is gentler than a slicker brush.

Metal Comb: Steel teeth attached to a steel handle; the closeness and size of the teeth vary greatly. A "flea comb" has tiny teeth set very closely together and is used to find fleas in a dog's coat. Combs with wider teeth are used for detangling longer coats.

Rake: Long-toothed comb with a short handle. Used to remove undercoat from heavily coated breeds with dense undercoats.

Soft-bristle Brush: Nylon or natural bristles set in a plastic or wood base. Used on short coats or long coats (without undercoats).

Rubber Curry: Rubber prongs, with or without a handle. Used for short-coated dogs. Good for use during shampooing.

Combination Brush: Two-sided brush with a different type of bristle on each side; for example, pin brush on one side and slicker on the other, or bristle brush on one side and pin brush on the other. An economical choice if you need two kinds of brushes.

Grooming Glove: Sometimes called a hound glove; used to give sleek-coated dogs a once-over.

Make sure he is at ease in the tub and have the water at a comfortable temperature. Begin bathing by wetting the coat all the way down to the skin. Massage in the shampoo, keeping it away from his face and eyes. Rinse him thoroughly, again avoiding the eyes and ears, as you don't want to get water into the ear canals. A thorough rinsing is important, as shampoo residue is drying and itchy to the dog. After rinsing, wrap him in a towel to absorb the initial moisture. You can finish drying with either a towel or a blow dryer on low heat, held at a safe distance from the dog. You should keep the dog indoors and away from drafts until he is completely dry.

Nail Clipping

Having his nails trimmed is not on many dogs' lists of favorite things to do. With this in mind, you will need to accustom your

> **SCOOTING HIS BOTTOM**
>
> Here's a problem that many owners tend to neglect. If your dog is scooting his rear end around the carpet, he probably is experiencing anal-sac impaction or blockage. The anal sacs are the two grape-sized glands on either side of the dog's vent. The dog cannot empty these glands, which become filled with a foul-smelling material. The dog may attempt to lick the area to relieve the pressure. He may also rub his anus on your walls, furniture or floors.
>
> Don't neglect your dog's rear end during grooming sessions. By squeezing both sides of the anus with a soft cloth, you can express some of the material in the sacs. If the material is pasty and thick, you likely will need the assistance of a veterinarian. Vets know how to express the glands and can show you how to do it correctly without hurting the dog or spraying yourself with the unpleasant liquid.

Begin trimming your Gordon's nails as a pup so that he tolerates his pedicures as an adult.

puppy to the procedure at a young age so that he will sit still (well, as still as he can) for his pedicures. Long nails can cause the dog's feet to spread, which is not good for him; likewise, long nails can hurt if they unintentionally scratch, not good for you!

Some dogs' nails are worn down naturally by regular walking on hard surfaces, so the frequency with which you clip depends on

The hair growing between the pads on the bottom of the feet should be trimmed short for neatness and to prevent discomfort to the dog.

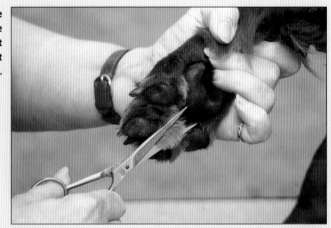

Excess hair around the foot should also be trimmed to present a tidy appearance.

The foot on the left is ungroomed; the foot on the right has been tidied up. Look at the difference!

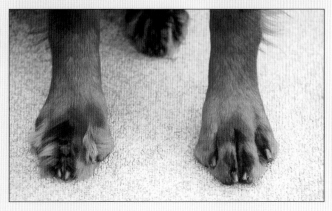

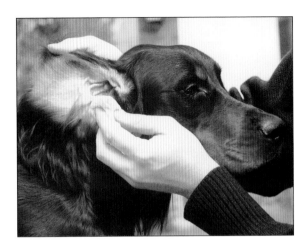

The Gordon's ears, being large and long, require regular cleaning. A cotton wipe, a specially formulated ear cleaner and a gentle touch should do the trick.

your individual dog. Look at his nails from time to time and clip as needed; a good way to know when it's time for a trim is if you hear your dog clicking as he walks across the floor.

There are several types of nail clippers and even electric nail-grinding tools made for dogs; first we'll discuss using the clipper. To start, have your clipper ready and some doggie treats on hand. You want your pup to view his nail-clipping sessions in a positive light, and what better way to convince him than with food? You may want to enlist the help of an assistant to comfort the pup and offer treats as you concentrate on the clipping itself. The guillotine-type clipper is thought of by many as the easiest type to use; the nail tip is inserted into the opening, and blades on the top and bottom snip it off in one clip.

Start by grasping the pup's paw; a little pressure on the foot pad causes the nail to extend, making it easier to clip. Clip off a little at a time. If you can see the "quick," which is a blood vessel that runs through each nail, you will know how much to trim, as you do not want to cut into the quick. On that note, if you do cut the quick, which will cause bleeding, you can stem the flow of blood with a styptic pencil or other clotting agent. If you mistakenly nip the quick, do not panic or fuss, as this will cause the pup to be afraid. Simply reassure the pup, stop the bleeding and move on to the next nail. Don't be discouraged; you will become a professional canine pedicurist with practice.

You may or may not be able to see the quick, so it's best to just clip off a small bit at a time. If you see a dark dot in the center of the nail, this is the quick and your cue to stop clipping. Tell the puppy he's a "good boy" and offer a piece of treat with each nail. You can also use nail-clipping time to examine the footpads, making sure that they are not dry and cracked and that nothing has become embedded in them.

The nail grinder, the other choice, is many owners' first choice. Accustoming the puppy to the sound of the grinder and sensation of the buzz presents fewer challenges than the clipper, and there's no chance of cutting through the quick. Use the grinder on a low setting and always talk soothingly to your dog. He won't mind his salon visit, and he'll have nicely polished nails as well.

EAR CLEANING

While keeping your dog's ears clean unfortunately will not cause him to "hear" your commands any better, it will protect him from ear infection and ear-mite infestation. In addition, a dog's ears are vulnerable to waxy build-up and to collecting foreign matter from the outdoors. Look in your dog's ears regularly to ensure that they look pink, clean and otherwise healthy. Even if they look fine, an odor in the ears signals a problem and means it's time to call the vet.

A dog's ears should be cleaned regularly; once a week is suggested, and you can do this along with your regular brushing. Using a cotton ball or pad, and never probing into the ear canal, wipe the ear gently. You can use an ear-cleansing liquid or powder available from your vet or pet-supply store; alternatively, you might prefer to use home-made solutions with ingredients like one part white vinegar and one part hydrogen peroxide. Ask your vet about home remedies before you attempt to concoct something on your own!

Keep your dog's ears free of excess hair by plucking it as

The area around the eyes can be cleaned using a special cleaner sold in pet-supply stores expressly for this purpose.

needed. If done gently, this will be painless for the dog. Look for wax, brown droppings (a sign of ear mites), redness or any other abnormalities. At the first sign of a problem, contact your vet so that he can prescribe an appropriate medication.

EYE CARE

During grooming sessions, pay extra attention to the condition of your dog's eyes. If the area around the eyes is soiled or if tear staining has occurred, there are various cleaning agents made especially for this purpose. Look at the dog's eyes to make sure no debris has entered; dogs with large eyes and those who spend time outdoors are especially prone to this.

The signs of an eye infection are obvious: mucus, redness, puffiness, scabs or other signs of irritation. If your dog's eyes become infected, the vet will likely prescribe an antibiotic oint-

Your Gordon is a precious family member, so you always do your best to provide for his safety and well-being.

ment for treatment. If you notice signs of more serious problems, such as opacities in the eye, which usually indicate cataracts, consult the vet at once. Taking time to pay attention to your dog's eyes will alert you in the early stages of any problem so that you can get your dog treatment as soon as possible. You could save your dog's sight!

IDENTIFICATION AND TRAVEL

ID FOR YOUR DOG

You love your Gordon Setter and want to keep him safe. Of course you take every precaution to prevent his escaping from the yard or becoming lost or stolen. You have a sturdy high fence and you always keep your dog on lead when out and about in public places. If your dog is not properly identified, however, you are overlooking a major aspect of his safety. We hope to never be in a situation where our dog is missing, but we should practice prevention in the unfortunate case that this happens; identification greatly increases the chances of your dog's being returned to you.

There are several ways to identify your dog. First, the traditional dog tag should be a staple in your dog's wardrobe, attached to his everyday collar. Tags can be made of sturdy plastic and various metals and should include your contact information so that a person who finds the dog can get in touch with you right away to arrange his return. Many people today enjoy the wide range of decorative tags available, so have fun and create a tag to match your dog's personality. Of course, it is important that the tag stays on the collar, so have a secure "O" ring attachment; you also can explore the type of tag that slides right onto the collar.

In addition to the ID tag, which every dog should wear even if identified by another method, two other forms of identification have become popular:

PET OR STRAY?

Besides the obvious benefit of providing your contact information to whoever finds your lost dog, an ID tag makes your dog more approachable and more likely to be recovered. A strange dog wandering the neighborhood without a collar and tags will look like a stray, while the collar and tags indicate that the dog is someone's pet. Even if the ID tags become detached from the collar, the collar alone will make a person more likely to pick up the dog.

microchipping and tattooing. In microchipping, a tiny scannable chip is painlessly inserted under the dog's skin. The number is registered to you so that, if your lost dog turns up at a clinic or shelter, the chip can be scanned to retrieve your contact information.

The advantage of the microchip is that it is a permanent form of ID, but there are some factors to consider. Several different companies make microchips, and not all are compatible with the others' scanning devices. It's best to find a company with a universal microchip that can be read by scanners made by other companies as well. It won't do any good to have the dog chipped if the information cannot be retrieved. Also, not every humane society, shelter and clinic is

equipped with a scanner, although more and more facilities are equipping themselves. In fact, many shelters microchip dogs that they adopt out to new homes.

Because the microchip is not visible to the eye, the dog must wear a tag that states that he is microchipped so that whoever picks him up will know to have him scanned. Most microchip tags list the dog's microchip number and the registry's phone number in case his chip cannot be read. He of course should also wear a tag with his owner's contact information. Humane societies and veterinary clinics offer microchipping service, which is usually very affordable.

Though less popular than microchipping, tattooing is another permanent method of ID for dogs. Most vets perform this service, and there are also clinics that perform dog tattooing. This is also an affordable procedure and one that will not cause much discomfort for the dog. It is best to put the tattoo in a visible area, such as the ear, to deter theft. It is sad to say that there are cases of dogs' being stolen and sold to research laboratories, but such laboratories will not accept tattooed dogs.

To ensure that the tattoo is effective in aiding your dog's return to you, the tattoo number must be registered with a national organization. That way, when

For safety's sake, never permit your Gordon to roam freely in a moving vehicle. Your dog's crate, a seat belt made for dogs and safety gates (shown here) are good options for restraint during travel.

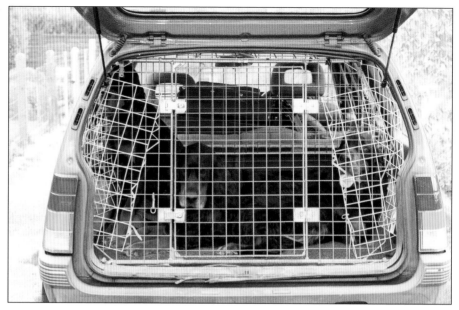

For safety's sake, never permit your Gordon to roam freely in a moving vehicle. Your dog's crate, a seat belt made for dogs and safety gates (shown here) are good options for restraint during travel.

someone finds a tattooed dog, a phone call to the registry will quickly match the dog with his owner.

HIT THE ROAD

Car travel with your Gordon Setter may be limited to necessity only, such as trips to the vet, or you may bring your dog along almost everywhere you go. This will depend much on your individual dog and how he reacts to rides in the car. You can begin desensitizing your dog to car travel as a pup so that it's something that he's used to. Still, some dogs suffer from motion sickness. Your vet may prescribe a medication for this if trips in the car pose a problem for your

dog. At the very least, you will need to get him to the vet, so he will need to tolerate these trips with the least amount of hassle possible.

Start taking your pup on short trips, maybe just around the block to start. If he is fine with short trips, lengthen your rides a little at a time. Start to take him on your errands or just for drives around town. By this time it will be easy to tell whether your dog is a born traveler or would prefer staying at home when you are on the road.

Of course, safety is a concern for dogs in the car. First, he must travel securely, not left loose to roam about the car where he could be injured or distract the driver. A young pup can be held by a passenger initially but should soon graduate to a travel crate, which can be the same crate he uses in the home if your vehicle can accommodate a Gordon-sized crate. Other options include a car harness (like a seat belt for dogs) and partitioning the back of the car with a gate made for this purpose.

Bring along what you will need for the dog. He should wear his collar and ID tags, of course, and you should bring his leash, water (and food if a long trip) and clean-up materials for potty breaks and in case of motion sickness. Always keep your dog on his leash when you make stops, and never leave him alone in the car. Many a dog has died from the heat inside a closed car; this does

DOGGONE!
Wendy Ballard is the editor and publisher of the *DogGone*™ newsletter, which comes out bi-monthly and features fun articles by dog owners who love to travel with their dogs. The newsletter includes information about fun places to go with your dogs, including popular vacation spots, dog-friendly hotels, parks, campgrounds, resorts, etc., as well as interesting activities to do with your dog, such as flyball, agility and much more. You can subscribe to the publication by contacting the publisher at PO Box 651155, Vero Beach, FL 32965-1155.

not take much time at all. A dog left alone inside a car can also be a target for thieves.

You should investigate the boarding facilities in your area so that you can choose one with which you are comfortable well before you need it.

BASIC TRAINING PRINCIPLES: PUPPY VS. ADULT

There's a big difference between training an adult dog and training a young puppy. With a young puppy, everything is new! At eight to ten weeks of age, he will be experiencing many things, and he has nothing with which to compare these experiences. Up to this point, he has been with his dam and littermates, not one-on-one with people except in his interactions with his breeder and visitors to the litter.

When you first bring the puppy home, he is eager to please you. This means that he accepts doing things your way. During the next couple of months, he will absorb the basis of everything he needs to know for the rest of his life. This early age is even referred to as the "sponge" stage. After that, for the next 18 months, it's up to you to reinforce good manners by building on the foundation that you've established. Once your puppy is reliable in basic commands and behavior and has reached the appropriate age, you may gradually introduce him to some of the interesting sports,

A properly trained Gordon Setter is a calm and delightful dog, eager to please his master and an enjoyable companion.

BASIC PRINCIPLES OF DOG TRAINING

1. Start training early. A young puppy is ready, willing and able.
2. Timing is your all-important tool. Praise at the exact time that the dog responds correctly. Pay close attention.
3. Patience is almost as important as timing!
4. Repeat! The same word has to mean the same thing every time.
5. In the beginning, praise all correct behavior verbally, along with treats and petting.

games and activities available to pet owners and their dogs.

Raising your puppy is a family affair. Each member of the family must know what rules to set forth for the puppy and how to use the same one-word commands to mean exactly the same thing every time. Even if yours is a large family, one person will soon be considered by the pup to be the leader, the alpha person in his pack, the "boss" who must be obeyed. Often that highly regarded person turns out to be the one who feeds the puppy. Food ranks very high on the puppy's list of important things! That's why your puppy is rewarded with small treats along with verbal praise when he responds to you correctly. As the puppy learns to do what you want him to do, the food rewards are gradually eliminated and only the praise remains. If you were to keep up with the food treats, you could have two problems on your hands—an obese dog and a beggar.

Gordon Setters are known to be sensitive dogs who learn best with gentle but consistent teaching methods. They thrive on praise and knowing that they have pleased their masters. Physical punishment is inappropriate for any breed and will certainly teach a Gordon to be afraid of his owner.

Training begins the minute your Gordon Setter puppy steps through the doorway of your home, so don't make the mistake of putting the puppy on the floor and telling him by your actions to "Go for it! Run wild!" Even if this

KEEP IT SIMPLE—AND FUN

Practicing obedience is not a military drill. Keep your lessons simple, interesting and user-friendly. Fun breaks help you both. Spend two minutes or ten teaching your puppy, but practice only as long as your dog enjoys what he's doing and is focused on pleasing you. If he's bored or distracted, stop the training session after any correct response (always end on a high note!). After a few minutes of playtime, you can go back to "hitting the books."

is your first puppy, you must act as if you know what you're doing: be the boss. An uncertain pup may be terrified to move, while a bold one will be ready to take you at your word and start plotting to destroy the house! Before you collected your puppy, you decided where his own special place would be, and that's where

TEACHER'S PET

Dogs are individuals, not robots, with many traits basic to their breed. Some, bred to work alone, are independent thinkers; others rely on you to call the shots. If you have enrolled in a training class, your instructor can offer alternative methods of training based on your individual dog's instincts and personality. You may benefit from using a different type of collar or switching to a class with different kinds of dogs.

to put him when you first arrive home. Give him a house tour after he has investigated his area and had a nap and a bathroom "pit stop."

It's worth mentioning here that, if you've adopted an adult dog that is completely trained to your liking, lucky you! You're off the hook! However, if that dog spent his life up to this point in a kennel, or even in a good home but without any real training, be prepared to tackle the job ahead. A dog three years of age or older with no previous training cannot be blamed for not knowing what he was never taught. While the dog is trying to understand and learn your rules, at the same time he has to unlearn many of his previously self-taught habits and general view of the world.

Working with a professional trainer will speed up your progress with an adopted adult dog. You'll need patience, too. Some new rules may be close to impossible for the dog to accept. After all, he's been successful so far by doing everything his way! (Patience again.) He may agree with your instruction for a few days and then slip back into his old ways, so you must be just as consistent and understanding in your teaching as you would be with a puppy. (More patience needed yet again!) Your dog has to learn to pay attention to your voice, your family, the daily routine, new smells, new sounds and, in some cases, even a new climate.

One of the most important things to find out about a newly adopted adult dog is his reaction to children (yours and others), strangers and your friends, and how he acts upon meeting other dogs. If he was not socialized with dogs as a puppy, this could be a major problem. This does not mean that he's a "bad" dog, a vicious dog or an aggressive dog; rather, it means that he has no idea how to read another dog's body language. There's no way for him to tell whether the other dog is a friend or foe. Survival instinct takes over, telling him to attack first and ask questions later. This definitely calls for professional help and, even then, may not be a behavior that can be corrected 100% reliably (or even at all). If you have a puppy, this is why it is so very important to introduce your young puppy properly to other puppies and "dog-friendly" adult dogs.

HOUSE-TRAINING YOUR GORDON SETTER

Dogs are tactility-oriented when it comes to house-training. In other words, they respond to the surface on which they are given approval to eliminate. The choice is yours (the dog's version is in parentheses): The lawn (including the neighbors' lawns)? A bare patch of earth under a tree (where people like to sit and relax in the summertime)? Concrete steps or patio (all sidewalks, garages and basement floors)? The curbside (watch out for cars)? A small area of crushed stone in a corner of the yard (mine!)? The latter is the best choice if you can manage it because it will remain strictly for the dog's use and is easy to keep clean.

You can start out with paper-training indoors and switch over to an outdoor surface as the puppy matures and gains control over his need to eliminate. For the nay-sayers, don't worry—this won't mean that the dog will soil on every piece of newspaper lying around the house. You are training him to go outside, remember? Starting out by paper-training often is the only choice for a city dog.

SHOULD WE ENROLL?
If you have the means and the time, you should definitely take your dog to obedience classes. Begin with puppy kindergarten classes in which puppies of all sizes learn basic lessons while getting the opportunity to meet and greet each other; it's as much about socialization as it is about good manners. What you learn in class, you can practice at home. And if you goof up in practice, you'll get help in the next session.

a dog-sitter or ask a neighbor to come over to take the pup outside, feed him his lunch and then take him out again about ten or so minutes after he's eaten. Also

> **EXTRA! EXTRA!**
> The headlines read: "Puppy Piddles Here!" Breeders commonly use newspapers to line their whelping pens, so puppies learn to associate newspapers with relieving themselves. Do not use newspapers to line your pup's crate, as this will signal to your puppy that it is OK to urinate in his crate. If you choose to paper-train your puppy, you will layer newspapers on a section of the floor near the door he uses to go outside. You should encourage the puppy to use the papers to relieve himself, and bring him there whenever you see him getting ready to go. Little by little, you will reduce the size of the newspaper-covered area so that the puppy will learn to relieve himself "on the other side of the door."

The basic principle of toilet training is that what goes in must come out. Adults can "hold it" for much longer than puppies and usually need about four daily potty trips.

WHEN YOUR PUPPY'S "GOT TO GO"

Your puppy's need to relieve himself is seemingly non-stop, but signs of improvement will be seen each week. From 8 to 10 weeks old, the puppy will have to be taken outside every time he wakes up, about 10–15 minutes after every meal and after every period of play—all day long, from first thing in the morning until his bedtime! That's a total of ten or more trips per day to teach the puppy where it's okay to relieve himself. With that schedule in mind, you can see that house-training a young puppy is not a part-time job. It requires someone to be home all day.

If that seems overwhelming or impossible, do a little planning. For example, plan to pick up your puppy at the start of a vacation period. If you can't get home in the middle of the day, plan to hire

make arrangements with that or another person to be your "emergency" contact if you have to stay late on the job. Remind yourself—repeatedly—that this hectic schedule improves as the puppy gets older.

HOME WITHIN A HOME

Your Gordon Setter puppy needs to be confined to one secure, puppy-proof area when no one is able to watch his every move. Generally, the kitchen is the place of choice because the floor is washable. Likewise, it's a busy family area that will accustom the pup to a variety of noises, everything from pots and pans to the telephone, blender and dishwasher. He will also be enchanted by the smell of your cooking (and will never be critical when you burn something). An exercise pen (also called an "ex-pen," a puppy version of a playpen) within the room of choice is an excellent means of confinement for a young pup. He can see out and has a certain amount of space in which to run about, but he is safe from dangerous things like electrical cords, heating units, trash baskets and open kitchen-supply cabinets. Place the pen where the puppy will not get a blast of heat or air conditioning.

In the pen, you can put a few toys, his bed (which can be his crate if the dimensions of pen and

BE UPSTANDING!

You are the dog's leader. During training, stand up straight so your dog looks up at you, and therefore up *to* you. Say the command words distinctly, in a clear, declarative tone of voice. (No barking!) Give rewards only as the correct response takes place (remember your timing!). Praise, smiles and treats are "rewards" used to positively reinforce correct responses. Don't repeat a mistake. Just change to another exercise—you will soon find success!

crate are compatible) and a few layers of newspaper in one small corner, just in case. A water bowl can be hung at a convenient height on the side of the ex-pen so it won't become a splashing pool for an innovative puppy. His food

A wire crate with soft padding gives puppy a comfortable spot where he can feel part of his surroundings while staying safe and learning the potty routine.

to hear those wake-up yips in the morning, put the crate in a corner of your bedroom. However, don't make any response whatsoever to whining or crying. If he's completely ignored, he'll settle down and get to sleep.

Good bedding for a young puppy is an old folded bath towel or an old blanket, something that is easily washable and disposable if necessary ("accidents" will happen!). Never put newspaper in the puppy's crate. Also, those old ideas about adding a clock to replace his mother's heartbeat, or a hot-water bottle to replace her warmth, are just that—old ideas. The clock could drive the puppy nuts, and the hot-water bottle could end up as a very soggy

dish can go on the floor, next to the water bowl.

Crates are something that pet owners are at last getting used to for their dogs. Wild or domestic canines have always preferred to sleep in den-like safe spots, and that is exactly what the crate provides. How often have you seen adult dogs that choose to sleep under a table or chair even though they have full run of the house? It's the den connection.

In your "happy" voice, use the word "Crate" every time you put the pup into his den. If he's new to a crate, toss in a small biscuit for him to chase the first few times. At night, after he's been outside, he should sleep in his crate. The crate may be kept in his designated area at night or, if you want to be sure

DAILY SCHEDULE
How many relief trips does your puppy need per day? A puppy up to the age of 14 weeks will need to go outside about 8 to 12 times per day! You will have to take the pup out any time he starts sniffing around the floor or turning in small circles, as well as after naps, meals, games and lessons or whenever he's released from his crate. Once the puppy is 14 to 22 weeks of age, he will require only 6 to 8 relief trips. At the ages of 22 to 32 weeks, the puppy will require about 5 to 7 trips. Adult dogs typically require 4 relief trips per day, in the morning, afternoon, evening and late at night.

CANINE DEVELOPMENT SCHEDULE

It is important to understand how and at what age a puppy develops into adulthood.
If you are a puppy owner, consult this Canine Development Schedule to
determine the stage of development your puppy is currently experiencing.
This knowledge will help you as you work with the puppy in the weeks and months ahead.

PERIOD	AGE	CHARACTERISTICS
FIRST TO THIRD	BIRTH TO SEVEN WEEKS	Puppy needs food, sleep and warmth and responds to simple and gentle touching. Needs mother for security and disciplining. Needs littermates for learning and interacting with other dogs. Pup learns to function within a pack and learns pack order of dominance. Begin socializing pup with adults and children for short periods. Pup begins to become aware of his environment.
FOURTH	EIGHT TO TWELVE WEEKS	Brain is fully developed. Pup needs socializing with outside world. Remove from mother and littermates. Needs to change from canine pack to human pack. Human dominance necessary. Fear period occurs between 8 and 12 weeks. Avoid fright and pain.
FIFTH	THIRTEEN TO SIXTEEN WEEKS	Training and formal obedience should begin. Less association with other dogs, more with people, places, situations. Period will pass easily if you remember this is pup's change-to-adolescence time. Be firm and fair. Flight instinct prominent. Permissiveness and over-disciplining can do permanent damage. Praise for good behavior.
JUVENILE	FOUR TO EIGHT MONTHS	Another fear period about seven to eight months of age. It passes quickly, but be cautious of fright and pain. Sexual maturity reached. Dominant traits established. Dog should understand sit, down, come and stay by now.

NOTE: THESE ARE APPROXIMATE TIME FRAMES. ALLOW FOR INDIVIDUAL DIFFERENCES IN PUPPIES.

waterbed! An extremely good breeder would have introduced your puppy to the crate by letting two pups sleep together for a couple of nights, followed by several nights alone. How thankful you will be if you found that breeder!

Safe toys in the pup's crate or area will keep him occupied, but monitor their condition closely. Discard any toys that show signs of being chewed to bits. Squeaky parts, bits of stuffing or plastic or any other small pieces can cause intestinal blockage or possibly choking if swallowed.

PROGRESSING WITH POTTY-TRAINING
After you've taken your puppy out and he has relieved himself in the area you've selected, he can have some free time with the family as long as there is someone responsible for watching him. That doesn't mean just someone in the same room who is watching TV or busy on the computer, but one person who is doing nothing other than keeping an eye on the pup, playing with him on the floor and helping him understand his position in the pack.

This first taste of freedom will let you begin to set the house rules. If you don't want the dog on the furniture, now is the time to prevent his first attempts to jump up onto the couch. The word to use in this case is "Off," not "Down." "Down" is the word you will use to teach the down position, which is something entirely different.

Most corrections at this stage come in the form of simply distracting the puppy. Instead of telling him "No" for "Don't chew the carpet," distract the chomping puppy with a toy and he'll forget about the carpet.

As you are playing with the pup, do not forget to watch him closely and pay attention to his body language. Whenever you see him begin to circle or sniff, take the puppy outside to relieve himself. If you are paper-training, put him back into his confined area on the newspapers. In either case, praise him as he eliminates

POTTY COMMAND
Most dogs love to please their masters; there are no bounds to what dogs will do to make their owners happy. The potty command is a good example of this theory. If toileting on command makes the master happy, then more power to him. Puppies will obligingly piddle if it really makes their keepers smile. Some owners can be creative about which word they will use to command their dogs to relieve themselves. Some popular choices are "Potty," "Tinkle," "Piddle," "Let's go," "Hurry up" and "Toilet." Give the command every time your puppy goes into position and the puppy will begin to associate his business with the command.

while he actually is *in the act* of relieving himself. Three seconds after he has finished is too late! You'll be praising him for running toward you, picking up a toy or whatever he may be doing at that moment, and that's not what you want to be praising him for. Timing is a vital tool in all dog training. Use it!

Remove soiled newspapers immediately and replace them

SOMEBODY TO BLAME

House-training a puppy can be frustrating for the puppy and the owner alike. The puppy does not instinctively understand the difference between defecating on the pavement outside and on the ceramic tile in the kitchen. He is confused and frightened by his human's exuberant reactions to his natural urges. The owner, arguably the more intelligent of the duo, is also frustrated that he cannot convince his puppy to obey his commands and instructions.

In frustration, the owner may struggle with the temptation to discipline the puppy, scold him or even strike him on the rear end. Harsh corrections are unnecessary and inappropriate, serving to defeat your purpose in gaining your puppy's trust and respect. Don't blame your nine-week-old puppy. Blame yourself for not being 100% consistent in the puppy's lessons and routine. The lesson here is simple: try harder and your puppy will succeed.

with clean ones. You may want to take a small piece of soiled paper and place it in the middle of the new clean papers, as the scent will attract him to that spot when it's time to go again. That scent attraction is why it's so important to clean up any messes made in the house by using a product specially made to eliminate the odor of dog urine and droppings. Regular household cleansers won't do the trick. Pet shops sell the best pet deodorizers. Invest in the largest container you can find.

Scent attraction eventually will lead your pup to his chosen spot outdoors; this is the basis of outdoor training. When you take your puppy outside to relieve himself, use a one-word command such as "Outside" or "Go-potty" (that's one word to the puppy!) as

An exercise pen, high enough so that your pup can't climb out and sturdy enough that he can't knock it over, is a helpful tool for safe confinement.

circling. By careful observation, you'll soon work out a successful schedule.

Accidents, by the way, are just that—accidents. Clean them up quickly and thoroughly, without comment, after the puppy has been taken outside to finish his business and then put back into his area or crate. If you witness an accident in progress, say "No!" in a stern voice and get the pup outdoors immediately. No punishment is needed. You and your puppy are just learning each

Your dogs deserve a clean place to play, so always pick up any droppings in the yard immediately. You also must clean up after your dog in public places—it's the law.

you attach his leash. Then lead him to his spot. Now comes the hard part—hard for you, that is. Just stand there until he urinates and defecates. Move him a few feet in one direction or another if he's just sitting there looking at you, but remember that this is neither playtime nor time for a walk. This is strictly a business trip! Then, as he circles and squats (remember your timing!), give him a quiet "Good dog" as praise. If you start to jump for joy, ecstatic over his performance, he'll do one of two things: either he will stop mid-stream, as it were, or he'll do it again for you—in the house—and expect you to be just as delighted!

Give him five minutes or so and, if he doesn't go in that time, take him back indoors to his confined area and try again in another ten minutes, or immediately if you see him sniffing and

LEASH TRAINING

House-training and leash training go hand in hand, literally. When taking your puppy outside to do his business, lead him there on his leash. Unless an emergency potty run is called for, do not whisk the puppy up into your arms and take him outside. If you have a fenced yard, you have the advantage of letting the puppy loose to go out, but it's better to put the dog on the leash and take him to his designated place in the yard until he is reliably house-trained. Taking the puppy for a walk is the best way to house-train a dog. The dog will associate the walk with his time to relieve himself, and the exercise of walking stimulates the dog's bowels and bladder. Dogs that are not trained to relieve themselves on a walk may hold it until they get back home, which of course defeats half the purpose of the walk.

other's language, and sometimes it's easy to miss a puppy's message. Chalk it up to experience and watch more closely from now on.

KEEPING THE PACK ORDERLY

Discipline is a form of training that brings order to life. For example, military discipline is what allows the soldiers in an army to work as one. Discipline is a form of teaching and, in dogs, is the basis of how the successful pack operates. Each member knows his place in the pack and all respect the leader, or alpha dog. It is essential for your puppy that you establish this type of relationship, with you as the alpha, or leader. It is a form of social coexistence that all canines recognize and accept. Discipline, therefore, is never to be confused with punishment. When you teach your puppy how you want him to behave, and he behaves properly and you praise him for it, you are disciplining him with a form of positive reinforcement.

For a dog, rewards come in the form of praise, a smile, a cheerful tone of voice, a few friendly pats or a rub of the ears. Rewards are also small food treats. Obviously, that does not mean bits of regular dog food. Instead, treats are very small bits of special things like cheese or pieces of soft dog treats. The idea is to reward the dog with something very small that he can taste and swallow, providing instant positive reinforcement. If he has to take time to chew the treat, he will have forgotten what he did to earn it by the time he is finished!

Your puppy should never be physically punished. The displeasure shown on your face and in your voice is sufficient to signal to the pup that he has done something wrong. He wants to please everyone higher up on the social ladder, especially his leader, so a scowl and harsh voice will take care of the error. Growling out the word "Shame!" when the pup is caught in the act of doing something wrong is better than the repetitive "No." Some dogs hear "No" so often that they begin to think it's their name! By the way, do not use the dog's name when you're correcting him. His name is reserved to get his attention for something pleasant about to take place.

A future show dog must follow his handler's instructions. A large part of success in the ring is how the dog and person work together.

TIPS FOR TRAINING AND SAFETY

1. Whether on or off leash, practice only in a fenced area.
2. Remove the training collar when the training session is over.
3. Don't try to break up a dogfight.
4. "Come," "Leave it" and "Wait" are safety commands.
5. The dog belongs in a crate or behind a barrier when riding in the car.
6. Don't ignore the dog's first sign of aggression. Aggression only gets worse, so take it seriously.
7. Keep the faces of children and dogs separated.
8. Pay attention to what the dog is chewing.
9. Keep the vet's number near your phone.
10. "Okay" is a useful release command.

There are punishments that have nothing to do with you. For example, your dog may think that chasing cats is one reason for his existence. You can try to stop it as much as you like but without success, because it's such fun for the dog. But one good hissing, spitting swipe of a cat's claws across the dog's nose will put an end to the game forever. Intervene only when your dog's eyeball is seriously at risk. Cat scratches can cause permanent damage to an innocent but annoying puppy.

PUPPY KINDERGARTEN

COLLAR AND LEASH

Before you begin your Gordon Setter puppy's education, he must be used to his collar and leash. Choose a collar for your puppy that is secure, but not heavy or bulky. He won't enjoy training if he's uncomfortable. A flat buckle collar is fine for everyday wear and for initial puppy training. For older dogs, there are several types of training collars such as the martingale, which is a double loop that tightens slightly around the neck, or the head collar, which is similar to a horse's halter. When used properly, these types of collars are gentler and more effective than the traditional chain choke collar. The Gordon does not respond well to harsh physical means of training.

A lightweight 6-foot woven cotton or nylon training leash is preferred by most trainers because it is easy to fold up in your hand and comfortable to hold because there is a certain amount of give to it. There are lessons where the dog will start off 6 feet away from you at the end of the leash. The leash used to take the puppy outside to relieve himself is shorter because you don't want him to roam away from his area. The shorter leash will also be the one to use when you walk the puppy.

WHO'S TRAINING WHOM?

Dog training is a black-and-white exercise. The correct response to a command must be absolute, and the trainer must insist on completely accurate responses from the dog. A trainer cannot command his dog to sit and then settle for the dog's melting into the down position. Often owners are so pleased that their dogs "did something" in response to a command that they just shrug and say, "OK, down" even though they wanted the dog to sit. You want your dog to respond to the command without hesitation: he must respond at that moment and correctly every time.

If you've been wise enough to enroll in a puppy kindergarten training class, suggestions will be made as to the best collar and leash for your young puppy. I say "wise" because your puppy will be in a class with puppies in his age range (up to five months old) of all breeds and sizes. It's the perfect way for him to learn the right way (and the wrong way) to interact with other dogs as well as their people. You cannot teach your puppy how to interpret another dog's sign language. For a first-time puppy owner, these socialization classes are invaluable. For experienced dog owners, they are a real boon to further training.

Treats are used at all levels of training, from the backyard to the show ring, to motivate and reward.

ATTENTION

You've been using the dog's name since the minute you collected him from the breeder, so you should be able to get his attention by saying his name—with a big smile and in an excited tone of voice. His response will be the puppy equivalent of "Here I am! What are we going to do?" Your immediate response (if you haven't guessed by now) is "Good dog." Rewarding him at the moment he pays attention to you teaches him the proper way to respond when he hears his name.

EXERCISES FOR A BASIC CANINE EDUCATION

THE SIT EXERCISE

There are several ways to teach the puppy to sit. The first one is to catch him whenever he is about

Gentle pressure on the dog's rump will guide him into the correct position as he learns what you mean when you say "Sit."

> ## I WILL FOLLOW YOU
> Obedience isn't just a classroom activity. In your home you have many great opportunities to teach your dog polite manners. Allowing your pet on the bed or furniture elevates him to your level, which is not a good idea (the word is "Off!"). Use the "umbilical cord" method, keeping your dog on lead so he has to go with you wherever you go. You sit, he sits. You walk, he heels. You stop, he sit/stays. Everywhere you go, he's with you, but you go first!

to sit and, as his backside nears the floor, say "Sit, good dog!" That's positive reinforcement and, if your timing is sharp, he will learn that what he's doing at that second is connected to your saying "Sit" and that you think he's clever for doing it!

Another method is to start with the puppy on his leash in front of you. Show him a treat in the palm of your right hand. Bring your hand up under his nose and, almost in slow motion, move your hand up and back so his nose goes up in the air and his head tilts back as he follows the treat in your hand. At that point, he will have to either sit or fall over, so as his back legs buckle under, say "Sit, good dog," and then give him the treat and lots of praise. You may have to begin with your hand lightly running up his chest, actually lifting his chin up until he sits. Some (usually older) dogs require gentle pressure on their hindquarters with the left hand, in which case the dog should be on your left side. Puppies generally do not appreciate this physical dominance.

After a few times, you should be able to show the dog a treat in the open palm of your hand, raise your hand waist-high as you say "Sit" and have him sit. Once again, you have taught him two things at the same time. Both the verbal command and the motion of the hand are signals for the sit. Your puppy is watching you almost more than he is listening to you, so what you do is just as important as what you say.

Don't save any of these drills only for training sessions. Use them as much as possible at odd times during a normal day. The

READY, SIT, GO!
On your marks, get set: train! Most professional trainers agree that the sit command is the place to start your dog's formal education. Sitting is a natural posture for most dogs, and they respond to the sit exercise willingly and readily. For every lesson, begin with the sit command so that you start out with a successful exercise; likewise, you should practice the sit command at the end of every lesson as well because you always want to end on a high note.

dog should always sit before being given his food dish. He should sit to let you go through a doorway first, when the doorbell rings or when you stop to speak to someone on the street.

No matter the lesson, you want your Gordon Setter to be focused on the lesson and attentive to you.

THE DOWN EXERCISE
Before beginning to teach the down command, you must consider how the dog feels about this exercise. To him, "down" is a

Some dogs need a little more convincing when it comes to assuming the down position on command.

submissive position. Being flat on the floor with you standing over him is not his idea of fun. It's up to you to let him know that, while it may not be fun, the reward of your approval is worth his effort.

Start with the puppy on your left side in a sit position. Hold the leash right above his collar in your left hand. Have an extra-special treat, such as a small piece of cooked chicken or hot dog, in your right hand. Place it at the end of the pup's nose and steadily move your hand down and forward along the ground. Hold the leash to prevent a sudden lunge for the food. As the puppy goes into the down position, say "Down" very gently.

The difficulty with this exercise is twofold: it's both the submissive aspect and the fact that most people say the word "Down" as if they were drill sergeants in charge of recruits! So issue the command sweetly, give him the treat and have the pup maintain the down position for several seconds. If he tries to get up immediately, place your hands on his shoulders and press down gently, giving him a very quiet "Good dog." As you progress with this lesson, increase the "down time" until he will hold it until you say "Okay" (his cue for release). Practice this one in the house at various times throughout the day.

By increasing the length of time during which the dog must maintain the down position, you'll find many uses for it. For example, he can lie at your feet in the vet's office or anywhere that both of you have to wait, when you are on the phone, while the family is eating and so forth. If you progress to training for competitive obedience, he'll already be all set for the exercise called the "long down."

SAY IT SIMPLY

When you command your dog to sit, use the word "Sit." Do not say "Sit down," as your dog will not know whether you mean "Sit" or "Down," or maybe you mean both. Be clear in your instructions to your dog; use one-word commands and always be consistent.

Using hand signals in conjunction with verbal commands reinforces the command and also gives you a head start if you choose to proceed to competitive obedience.

THE STAY EXERCISE

You can teach your Gordon Setter to stay in the sit, down and stand positions. To teach the sit/stay,

> **OKAY!**
> This is the signal that tells your dog that he can quit whatever he was doing. Use "Okay" to end a session on a correct response to a command. (Never end on an incorrect response.) Lots of praise follows. People use "Okay" a lot and it has other uses for dogs, too. Your dog is barking. You say, "Okay! Come!" "Okay" signals him to stop the barking activity and "Come" allows him to come to you for a "Good dog."

have the dog sit on your left side. Hold the leash at waist level in your left hand and let the dog know that you have a treat in your closed right hand. Step forward on your right foot as you say "Stay." Immediately turn and stand directly in front of the dog, keeping your right hand up high so he'll keep his eye on the treat hand and maintain the sit position for a count of five. Return to your original position and offer the reward.

Increase the length of the sit/stay each time until the dog can hold it for at least 30 seconds without moving. After about a week of success, move out on your right foot and take two steps

Once your Gordon Setter is comfortable with the down command, you can progress to the down/stay.

before turning to face the dog. Give the "Stay" hand signal (left palm back toward the dog's head) as you leave. He gets the treat when you return and he holds the sit/stay. Increase the distance that you walk away from him before turning until you reach the length of your training leash. But don't rush it! Go back to the beginning if he moves before he should. No matter what the lesson, never be upset by having to back up for a few days. The repetition and practice are what will make your dog reliable in these commands. It won't do any good to move on to something more difficult if the command is not mastered at the easier levels. Above all, even if you do get frustrated, never let your puppy know! Always keep a positive, upbeat attitude during training, which will transmit to your dog for positive results.

The down/stay is taught in the same way once the dog is completely reliable and steady with the down command. Again, don't rush it. With the dog in the down position on your left side, step out on your right foot as you say "Stay." Return by walking around in back of the dog and into your original position. While you are training, it's okay to murmur something like "Hold on" to encourage him to stay put. When the dog will stay without moving when you are at a distance of 3 or 4 feet, begin to increase the length of time before you return. Be sure he holds the down on your return until you say "Okay." At that point, he gets his treat—just so he'll remember for next time that it's not over until it's over.

THE COME EXERCISE

No command is more important to the safety of your Gordon Setter than "Come." It is what you should say every single time you see the puppy running toward you: "Avery, come! Good dog." During playtime, run a few feet away from the puppy and turn and tell him to "Come" as he is already running to you. You can go so far as to teach your puppy two things at once if you squat down and hold out your arms. As the pup gets close to you and you're saying "Good dog," bring your right arm in about waist high. Now he's also learning the hand signal, an excellent device

Begin each new command with your dog on lead. Only progress to off-leash training in a securely enclosed area and only after the command has been mastered on lead.

TIME TO PLAY!

Playtime can happen both indoors and out. A young puppy is growing so rapidly that he needs sleep more than he needs a lot of physical exercise. Puppies get sufficient exercise on their own just through normal puppy activity. Monitor play with young children so you can remove the puppy when he's had enough, or calm the kids if they get too rowdy. Almost all puppies love to chase after a toy you've thrown, and you can turn your games into educational activities. Every time your puppy brings the toy back to you, say "Give it" (or "Drop it") followed by "Good dog" and throwing it again. If he's reluctant to give it to you, offer a small treat so that he drops the toy as he takes the treat. He will soon get the idea.

should you be on the phone when you need to get him to come to you! You'll also both be one step ahead when you enter obedience classes.

When the puppy responds to your well-timed "Come," try it with the puppy on the training leash. This time, catch him off-guard, while he's sniffing a leaf or watching a bird: "Avery, come!" You may have to pause for a split second after his name to be sure you have his attention. If the puppy shows any sign of confusion, give the leash a mild jerk and take a couple of steps backward. Do not repeat the command. In this case, you should say "Good come" as he reaches you.

That's the number-one rule of training. Each command word is

COME AND GET IT!
The come command is your dog's safety signal. Until he is 99% perfect in responding, don't use the come command if you cannot enforce it. Practice on leash with treats or squeakers, or whenever the dog is running to you. Never call him to come to you if he is to be corrected for a misdemeanor. Reward the dog with a treat and happy praise whenever he comes to you.

given just once. Anything more is nagging. You'll also notice that all commands are one word only. Even when they are actually two words, you say them as one.

Never call the dog to come to you—with or without his name—if you are angry or intend to correct him for some misbehavior. When correcting the pup, you go to him. Your dog must always connect "Come" with something pleasant and with your approval;

then you can rely on his response.

Puppies, like children, have notoriously short attention spans, so don't overdo it with any of the training. Keep each lesson short. Break it up with a quick run around the yard or a ball toss, repeat the lesson and quit as soon as the pup gets it right. That way, you will always end with a "Good dog."

Life isn't perfect and neither are puppies. A time will come, often around ten months of age, when he'll become "selectively deaf" or choose to "forget" his name. He may respond by wagging his tail (and even seeming to smile at you) with a look that says "Make me!" Laugh, throw his favorite toy and skip the lesson you had planned. Pups will be pups!

THE HEEL EXERCISE
The second most important command to teach, after the come, is the heel. When you are walking your growing puppy, you need to be in control. Besides, it looks terrible to be pulled and yanked down the street, and it's not much fun either. Your eight- to ten-week-old puppy will probably follow you everywhere, but that's his natural instinct, not your control over the situation. However, any time he does follow you, you can say "Heel" and be ahead of the game, as he will learn to associate this command

DON'T STRESS ME OUT
Your dog doesn't have to deal with paying the bills, the daily commute, PTA meetings and the like, but, believe it or not, there's a lot of stress in a dog's world. Stress can be caused by the owner's impatient demeanor and his angry or harsh corrections. If your dog cringes when you reach for his training collar, he's stressed. An older dog is sometimes stressed out when he goes to a new home. No matter what the cause, put off all training until he's over it. If he's going through a fear period—shying away from people, trembling when spoken to, avoiding eye contact or hiding under furniture—wait to resume training. Naturally you'd also postpone your lessons if the dog were sick, and the same goes for you. Show some compassion.

Retrieving games help reinforce the come command in the course of having fun.

with the action of following you before you even begin teaching him to heel.

There is a very precise, almost military, procedure for teaching your dog to heel. As with all other obedience training, begin with the dog on your left side. He will be in a very nice sit and you will have the training leash across your chest. Hold the loop and folded leash in your right hand. Pick up the slack leash above the dog in your left hand and hold it loosely at your side. Step out on your left foot as you say "Heel." If the puppy does not move, give a gentle tug or pat your left leg to get him started. If he surges ahead of you, stop and pull him back gently until he is at your side. Tell him to sit and begin again.

Walk a few steps and stop while the puppy is correctly beside you. Tell him to sit and give mild verbal praise. (More enthusiastic praise will encourage him to think the lesson is over.) Repeat the lesson, increasing the number of steps you take only as long as the dog is heeling nicely beside you. When you end the lesson, have him hold the sit, then give him the "Okay" to let him know that this is the end of the lesson. Praise him so that he knows he did a good job.

The cure for excessive pulling (a common problem) is to stop when the dog is no more than 2 or 3 feet ahead of you. Guide him back into position and begin again. With a really determined

Then start to give a treat after the end of only some of the lessons. At the end of every lesson, as well as during the lessons, be consistent with the praise. Your pup now doesn't know whether he'll get a treat or not, but he should keep performing well just in case! Finally, you will stop giving treat rewards entirely. Save them for

Gordons are active dogs that require stimulation and attention. Without sufficient exercise, a gundog like the Gordon can be distracted and high-strung, so it is much easier to train a dog that receives the activity he needs.

puller, try switching to a head collar. This will automatically turn the pup's head toward you so you can bring him back easily to the heel position. Give quiet, reassuring praise every time the leash goes slack and he's staying with you.

Staying and heeling can take a lot out of a dog, so provide playtime and free-running exercise to shake off the stress when the lessons are over. You don't want him to associate training with all work and no fun.

TAPERING OFF TIDBITS
Your dog has been watching you—and the hand that treats—throughout all of his lessons, and now it's time to break the treat habit. Begin by giving him treats at the end of each lesson only.

LET'S GO!
Many people use "Let's go" instead of "Heel" when teaching their dogs to behave on lead. It sounds more like fun! When beginning to teach the heel, whatever command you use, always step off on your left foot. That's the one next to the dog, who is on your left side, in case you've forgotten. Keep a loose leash. When the dog pulls ahead, stop, bring him back and begin again. Use treats to guide him around turns.

something brand-new that you want to teach him. Keep up the praise and you'll always have a "good dog."

OBEDIENCE CLASSES

The advantages of an obedience class are that your dog will have to learn amid the distractions of other people and dogs and that your mistakes will be quickly corrected by the trainer. Teaching your dog along with a qualified instructor and other handlers who may have more dog experience than you is another plus of the class environment. The instructor and other handlers can help you to find the most efficient way of teaching your dog a command or exercise. It's often easier to learn by other people's mistakes than your own. You will also learn all of the requirements for competitive obedience trials, in which you can earn titles and go on to advanced jumping and retrieving exercises, which are fun for many dogs. Obedience classes build the foundation needed for many other canine activities (in which we humans are allowed to participate, too!).

TRAINING FOR OTHER ACTIVITIES

Whether a dog is trained in the structured environment of a class or alone with his owner at home, there are many activities that can bring fun and rewards to both

owner and dog once they have mastered basic control.

Once your dog has basic obedience under his collar and is 12 months of age, you can enter

Bringing things to his owner comes naturally for the Gordon Setter. The breed has strong field instincts that can be developed for work or just for fun.

THE BEST INVESTMENT

Obedience school is as important for you and your dog as grammar school is for your kids, and it's a lot more fun! Don't shun classes thinking that your dog might embarrass you. He might! Instructors don't expect you to know everything, but they'll teach you the correct way to teach your dog so he won't embarrass you again. He'll become a social animal as you learn with other people and dogs. Home training, while effective in teaching your dog the basic commands, excludes these socialization benefits.

the world of agility training. Dogs think agility is pure fun, like being turned loose in an amusement park full of obstacles! In addition to agility, there are activities geared toward certain types of dogs, such as hunting activities for sporting dogs, like your Gordon, lure-coursing events for sighthounds, go-to-ground events for terriers, racing for the Nordic sled dogs, herding trials for the shepherd breeds and tracking, which is open to all "nosey" dogs (which would include all dogs!). For those who like to volunteer, there is the wonderful feeling of owning a therapy dog and visiting hospices, nursing homes and veterans' homes to bring smiles, comfort and companionship to those who live there.

Around the house, your Gordon Setter can be taught to do some simple chores. Teaching the dog to help out around the home, in the yard or on the farm provides great satisfaction to both dog and owner. In addition, the dog's help makes life a little easier for his owner and raises his stature as a valued companion to his family. It helps give the dog a purpose by occupying his mind and providing an outlet for his energy. You might teach him to carry a small basket of household items or to fetch the morning newspaper. The kids can teach the dog all kinds of tricks, from playing hide-and-seek to balancing a

biscuit on his nose. A family dog is what rounds out the family. Everything he does, including sitting at your feet or gazing lovingly at you, represents the bonus of owning a dog.

TRAINING FOR THE FIELD
If you've obtained a Gordon puppy with aspirations to work him in the field, he must be trained to do so. While hunting instincts are present in every well-bred Gordon Setter, you are better off starting out with a pup from proven field stock. But remember, no matter how many hunters and field titles are in the pedigree, the puppy won't learn on his own, and you must get started early. Early training takes advantage of the puppy's ability to

> **SMILE WHEN YOU ORDER ME AROUND!**
> While trainers recommend practicing with your dog every day, it's perfectly acceptable to take a "mental health day" off. It's better not to train the dog on days when you're in a sour mood. Your bad attitude or lack of interest will be sensed by your dog, and he will respond accordingly. Studies show that dogs are well tuned in to their humans' emotions. Be conscious of how you use your voice when talking to your dog. Raising your voice or shouting will only erode your dog's trust in you as his trainer and master.

learn quickly and also fosters a close bond with you from the start.

You will typically get started by introducing the pup to a wing of a bird. Usually this is attached to a rod and you playfully entice the dog to watch and chase after it. The next phase is to introduce the pup to an actual (dead) bird. At first, you want to make it easy for the pup to get the bird. He will be learning both to pick up the scent and to bring back the bird. You will progress from throwing the bird short distances, within the pup's sight, and encouraging him to retrieve it, to throwing it out of his sight, perhaps in tall grass, where he has to use his scenting ability to locate the bird.

After this phase, you will begin working with live birds. This is just a very brief outline of the field-training process. For all phases of field training, from beginning to advanced, you are advised to consult with an experienced field trainer or to join a field-training club. You will need advice about the procedures, what type of birds to use, how to create a safe and effective training location, how to encourage and reward your dog and much more. If this is your first field dog, you will definitely need assistance when it comes time to train your dog to the gun. Regardless of your level of experience, it is always

A born hunting dog, the Gordon Setter excels in many different gundog activities, from field trials to weekend hunting outings.

helpful to align yourself with a professional or with experienced fanciers to help you along the way and give you advice about any difficulties you may encounter.

Another option is that you do not intend to use your Gordon for field work, but you are interested in developing his natural instincts for competitive hunting and field events. You can start by visiting the AKC's website at www.akc.org and familiarizing yourself with how these events are organized. You will find trainers and clubs who can help you and your Gordon prepare for these types of competitions.

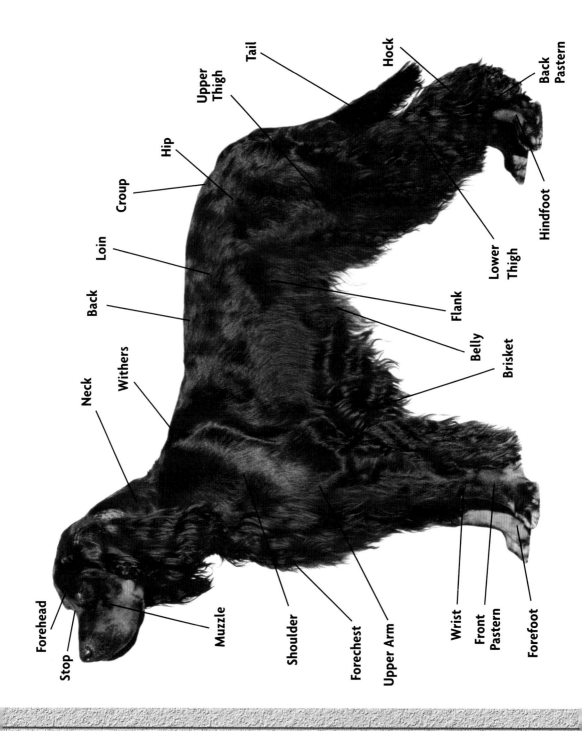

Forehead

Stop

Muzzle

Neck

Withers

Back

Loin

Croup

Hip

Upper Thigh

Tail

Hock

Back Pastern

Hindfoot

Lower Thigh

Flank

Belly

Brisket

Shoulder

Forechest

Upper Arm

Wrist

Front Pastern

Forefoot

PHYSICAL STRUCTURE OF THE GORDON SETTER

GORDON SETTER

BY LOWELL ACKERMAN DVM, DACVD

HEALTHCARE FOR A LIFETIME

When you own a dog, you become his healthcare advocate over his entire lifespan, as well as being the one to shoulder the financial burden of such care. Accordingly, it is worthwhile to focus on prevention rather than treatment, as you and your pet will both be happier.

Of course, the best place to have begun your program of preventive healthcare is with the initial purchase or adoption of your dog. There is no way of guaranteeing that your new furry friend is free of medical problems, but there are some things you can do to improve your odds. You certainly should have done adequate research into the Gordon Setter and have selected your puppy carefully rather than buying on impulse. Health issues aside, a large number of pet abandonment and relinquishment cases arise from a mismatch between pet needs and owner expectations. This is entirely preventable with appropriate planning and finding a good breeder.

Regarding healthcare issues specifically, it is very difficult to

Before you buy a dog, meet and interview the veterinarians in your area. Take everything into consideration; discuss background, specialties, fees, emergency policies, etc.

make blanket statements about where to acquire a problem-free pet, but, again, a reputable breeder is your best bet. In an ideal situation you have the opportunity to see both of the litter's parents, get references from other owners of the breeder's pups and see genetic-testing documentation for several generations of the litter's ancestors. At the very least, you must thoroughly investigate the Gordon Setter and the problems inherent in the breed, as well as the genetic testing available to screen for those problems. Genetic testing offers some important benefits, but testing is available for only a few disorders in a relatively small number of breeds and is not available for some of the most common

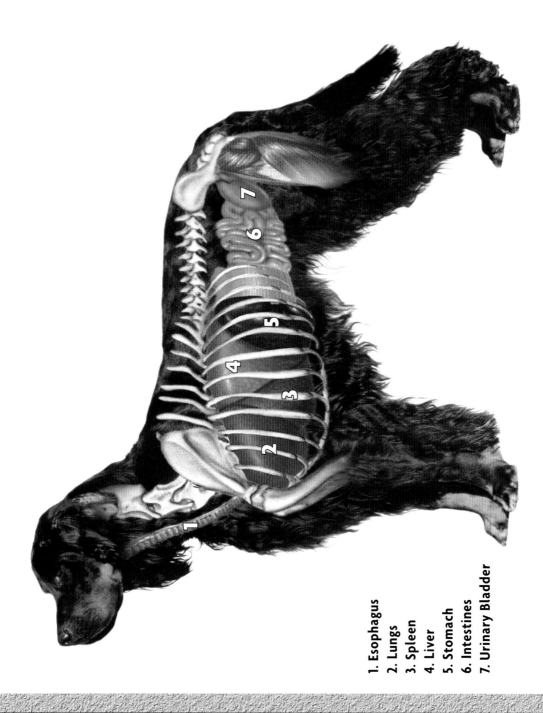

1. Esophagus
2. Lungs
3. Spleen
4. Liver
5. Stomach
6. Intestines
7. Urinary Bladder

INTERNAL ORGANS OF THE GORDON SETTER

genetic diseases, such as hip dysplasia, cataracts, epilepsy, cardiomyopathy, etc. This area of research is indeed exciting and increasingly important, and advances will continue to be made each year. In fact, recent research has shown that there is an equivalent dog gene for 75% of known human genes, so research done in either species is likely to benefit the other.

We've also discussed that evaluating the behavioral nature of your Gordon Setter and that of his immediate family members is an important part of the selection process that cannot be underestimated or overemphasized. It is sometimes difficult to evaluate temperament in puppies because certain behavioral tendencies, such as some forms of aggression, may not be immediately evident. More dogs are euthanized each year for behavioral reasons than for all medical conditions combined, so it is critical to take temperament issues seriously. Start with a well-balanced, friendly companion and put the time and effort into proper socialization, and you will both be rewarded with a longtime valued relationship.

Assuming that you have started off with a pup from healthy, sound stock, you then become responsible for helping your veterinarian keep your pet healthy. Some crucial things

happen before you even bring your puppy home. Parasite control typically begins at two weeks of age, and vaccinations typically begin at six to eight weeks of age. A pre-pubertal evaluation is typically scheduled for about six months of age. At this time, a dental evaluation is done (since the adult teeth are now in), heartworm prevention is started and neutering or spaying is most commonly done.

It is critical to commence regular dental care at home if you have not already done so. It may not sound very important, but most dogs have active periodontal disease by four years of age if they don't have their teeth cleaned regularly at home, not just at their veterinary exams. Dental problems lead to more than just bad "doggy breath." Gum disease can have very serious medical consequences. If you start brushing your dog's teeth and using antiseptic rinses from a young age,

Yes, you must brush your dog's teeth on a regular basis. Purchase a canine toothpaste and toothbrush at your local pet-supply shop. Brushing prevents tooth decay, bad breath and a multitude of more serious problems.

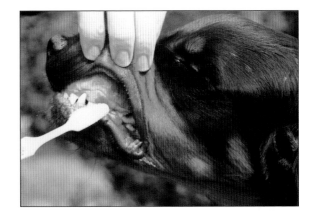

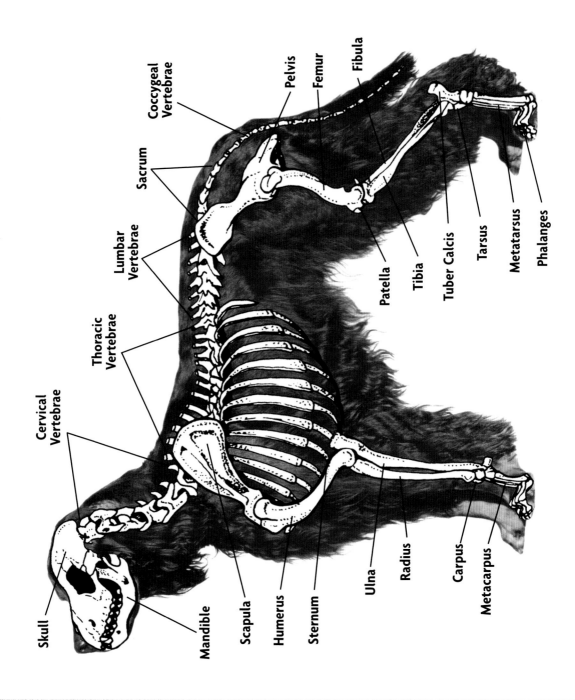

Coccygeal Vertebrae
Pelvis
Femur
Fibula

Sacrum

Lumbar Vertebrae

Thoracic Vertebrae

Cervical Vertebrae

Patella
Tibia
Tuber Calcis
Tarsus
Metatarsus
Phalanges

Skull
Mandible
Scapula
Humerus
Sternum
Ulna
Radius
Carpus
Metacarpus

SKELETAL STRUCTURE OF THE GORDON SETTER

your dog will be accustomed to it and will not resist. The results will be healthy dentition, which your pet will need to enjoy a long, healthy life.

Most dogs are considered adults at a year of age, although most larger breeds, like the Gordon, continue filling out for a couple of years. Even individual dogs within each breed have different healthcare requirements, so work with your veterinarian to determine what will be needed and what your role should be. This doctor-client relationship is important, because as vaccination guidelines change, there may not be an annual "vaccine visit" scheduled. You must make sure that you see your veterinarian at least annually, even if no vaccines are due, because this is the best opportunity to coordinate health-care activities and to make sure that no medical issues creep by unaddressed.

When your Gordon Setter reaches three-quarters of his antic-ipated lifespan, he is considered a "senior" and likely requires some special care. Your vet will sched-ule twice-yearly visits to catch any problems early on. In general, if you've been taking great care of your canine companion through-out his formative and adult years, the transition to senior status should be a smooth one. Age is not a disease, and as long as everything is functioning as it

should, there is no reason why most of late adulthood should not be rewarding for both you and your pet. This is especially true if you have tended to the details, such as regular veterinary visits, proper dental care, excellent nutrition and management of bone and joint issues.

SELECTING A VETERINARIAN

There is probably no more impor-tant decision that you will make regarding your pet's healthcare than the selection of his doctor. Your pet's veterinarian will be a pediatrician, family-practice physician and gerontologist, depending on the dog's life stage, and will be the individual who makes recommendations regard-ing issues such as when special-ists need to be consulted, when

THE WORRIES OF MANGE
Sometimes called "puppy mange," demodectic mange is passed to the puppy through the mother's milk. The microscopic mites that cause the condition take up residence in the puppy's hair follicles and sebaceous glands. Stress can cause the mites to multiply, causing bare patches on the face, neck and front legs. If neglected, it can lead to secondary bacterial infections, but if diagnosed and treated early, demodectic mange can be localized and controlled. Most pups recover without complications.

diagnostic testing and/or thera-peutic intervention is needed and when you will need to seek outside emergency and critical-care services. Your vet will act as your advocate and liaison throughout these processes.

Everyone has his own idea about what to look for in a vet, an individual who will play a big role in his dog's (and, of course, his own) life for many years to come. For some, it is the compas-sionate caregiver with whom they hope to develop a professional relationship to span the lives of their dogs and even their future pets. For others, they are seeking a clinician with keen diagnostic and therapeutic insight who can deliver state-of-the-art healthcare. Still others need a veterinary facility that is open evenings and weekends, is in close proximity or provides mobile veterinary services to accommodate their schedules; these people may not much mind that their dogs might see different veterinarians on each visit. Just as we have different reasons for selecting our own healthcare professionals (e.g., covered by insurance plan, expert in field, convenient location, etc.), we should not expect that there is a one-size-fits-all recommendation for selecting a veterinarian and veterinary practice. The best advice is to be honest in your assessment of what you expect from a veterinary practice and to conscientiously research the options in your area. You will quickly appreciate that not all veterinary practices are the same, and you will be happiest with one that truly meets your needs.

There is another point to be considered in the selection of veterinary services. Not that long ago, a single veterinarian would attempt to manage all medical and surgical issues as they arose. That was often problematic because veterinarians are trained in many

TAKING YOUR DOG'S TEMPERATURE

It is important to know how to take your dog's temperature at times when you think he may be ill. It's not the most enjoyable task, but it can be done without too much difficulty. It's easier with a helper, preferably someone with whom the dog is friendly, so that one of you can hold the dog while the other inserts the thermometer.

Before inserting the thermometer, coat the end with petroleum jelly. Insert the thermometer slowly and gently into the dog's rectum about one inch. Wait for the reading, about two minutes. Be sure to remove the thermometer carefully and clean it thoroughly after each use.

A dog's normal body temperature is between 100.5 and 102.5 degrees F. Immediate veterinary attention is required if the dog's temperature is below 99 or above 104 degrees F.

species and many diseases, and it was just impossible for general veterinary practitioners to be experts in every species, every field and every ailment. However, just as in the human healthcare fields, specialization has allowed general practitioners to concentrate on primary healthcare delivery, especially wellness and the prevention of infectious diseases, and to utilize a network of specialists to assist in the management of conditions that require specific expertise and experience. Thus there are now many types of veterinary specialists, including dermatologists, cardiologists, ophthalmologists, surgeons, internists, oncologists, neurologists, behaviorists, criticalists and others to help primary-care veterinarians deal with complicated medical challenges. In most cases, specialists see cases referred by primary-care veterinarians, make diagnoses and set up management plans. From there, the animals' ongoing care is returned to their primary-care veterinarians. This important team approach to your pet's medical-care needs has provided opportunities for advanced care and an unparalleled level of quality to be delivered.

With all of the opportunities for your Gordon Setter to receive high-quality veterinary medical care, there is another topic that needs to be addressed at the same time—cost. It's been said that you can have excellent healthcare or inexpensive healthcare, but never both; this is as true in veterinary

---

YOUR DOG NEEDS TO VISIT THE VET IF:

- He has ingested a toxin such as antifreeze or a toxic plant; in these cases, administer first aid and call the vet right away
- His teeth are discolored, loose or missing or he has sores or other signs of infection or abnormality in the mouth
- He has been vomiting, has had diarrhea or has been constipated for over 24 hours; call immediately if you notice blood
- He has refused food for over 24 hours
- His eating habits, water intake or toilet habits have noticeably changed; if you have noticed weight gain or weight loss
- He shows symptoms of bloat, which requires *immediate* attention
- He is salivating excessively
- He has a lump in his throat
- He has a lump or bumps anywhere on the body
- He is very lethargic
- He appears to be in pain or otherwise has trouble chewing or swallowing
- His skin loses elasticity

Of course, there will be other instances in which a visit to the vet is necessary; these are just some of the signs that could be indicative of serious problems that need to be caught as early as possible.

medicine as it is in human medicine. While veterinary costs are a fraction of what the same services cost in the human healthcare arena, it is still difficult to deal with unanticipated medical costs, especially since they can easily creep into hundreds or even thousands of dollars if specialists or emergency services become involved. However, there are ways of managing these risks. The easiest is to buy pet health insurance and realize that its foremost purpose is not to cover routine healthcare visits but rather to serve as an umbrella for those rainy days when your pet needs medical care and you don't want to worry about whether or not you can afford that care.

Pet insurance policies are very cost-effective (and very inexpensive by human health-insurance standards), but make sure that you buy the policy long before you intend to use it (preferably starting in puppyhood because coverage will exclude pre-existing conditions) and that you are actually buying an indemnity insurance plan from an insurance company that is regulated by your state or province. Many insurance policy look-alikes are actually discount clubs that are redeemable only at specific locations and for specific services. An indemnity plan covers your pet at almost all veterinary, specialty and emergency practices and is an excellent way to manage your pet's ongoing healthcare needs.

DENTAL WARNING SIGNS

A veterinary dental exam is necessary if you notice one or any combination of the following in your dog:

- Broken, loose or missing teeth
- Loss of appetite (which could be due to mouth pain or illness caused by infection)
- Gum abnormalities, including redness, swelling and bleeding
- Drooling, with or without blood
- Yellowing of the teeth or gumline, indicating tartar
- Bad breath

VACCINATIONS AND INFECTIOUS DISEASES

There has never been an easier time to prevent a variety of infectious diseases in your dog, but the advances we've made in veterinary medicine come with a price—choice. Now while it may seem that having choices about your pet's vaccinations is a good thing (and it is), it also has never been more difficult for the pet owner (or the veterinarian) to make an informed decision about the best way to protect pets through vaccination.

Years ago, it was just accepted that puppies got a starter series of vaccinations and then annual "boosters" throughout their lives to keep them protected. As more and more vaccines became available, consumers wanted the convenience of having all of that protection in a single injection. The result was "multivalent" vaccines that crammed a lot of protection into a single syringe. The manufacturers' recommendations were to give the vaccines annually, and this was a simple enough protocol to follow.

However, as veterinary medicine has become more sophisticated and we have started looking more at healthcare quandaries rather than convenience, it became necessary to reevaluate the situation and deal with some tough questions. It is important to realize that whether or not to use a particular vaccine depends on the risk of contracting the disease against which it protects, the severity of the disease if it is

contracted, the duration of immunity provided by the vaccine, the safety of the product and the needs of the individual animal. In a very general sense, rabies, distemper, hepatitis and parvovirus are considered core vaccine needs, while parain-

PROBLEM: AND THAT STARTS WITH "P"

Urinary tract problems more commonly affect female dogs, especially those who have been spayed. The first sign that a urinary tract problem exists usually is a strong odor from the urine or an unusual color. Blood in the urine, known as hematuria, is another sign of an infection, related to cystitis, a bladder infection, bladder cancer or a blood-clotting disorder. Urinary tract problems can also be signaled by the dog's straining while urinating, experiencing pain during urination and genital discharge as well as excessive water intake and urination.

Excessive drinking, in and of itself, does not indicate a urinary tract problem. A dog who is drinking more than normal may have a kidney or liver problem, a hormonal disorder or diabetes mellitus. Behaviorists report a disorder known as psychogenic polydipsia, which manifests itself in excessive drinking and urination. If you notice your dog drinking much more than normal, take him to the vet.

COMMON INFECTIOUS DISEASES

Let's discuss some of the diseases that create the need for vaccination in the first place. Following are the major canine infectious diseases and a simple explanation of each.

Rabies: A devastating viral disease that can be fatal in dogs and people. In fact, vaccination of dogs and cats is an important public-health measure to create a resistant animal buffer population to protect people from contracting the disease. Vaccination schedules are determined on a government level and are not optional for pet owners; rabies vaccination is required by law in all 50 states.

Parvovirus: A severe, potentially life-threatening disease that is easily transmitted between dogs. There are four strains of the virus, but it is believed that there is significant "cross-protection" between strains that may be included in individual vaccines.

Distemper: A potentially severe and life-threatening disease with a relatively high risk of exposure, especially in certain regions. In very high-risk distemper environments, young pups may be vaccinated with human measles vaccine, a related virus that offers cross-protection when administered at four to ten weeks of age.

Hepatitis: Caused by canine adenovirus type 1 (CAV-1), but since vaccination with the causative virus has a higher rate of adverse effects, cross-protection is derived from the use of adenovirus type 2 (CAV-2), a cause of respiratory disease and one of the potential causes of canine cough. Vaccination with CAV-2 provides long-term immunity against hepatitis, but relatively less protection against respiratory infection.

Canine cough: Also called tracheobronchitis, actually a fairly complicated result of viral and bacterial offenders; therefore, even with vaccination, protection is incomplete. Wherever dogs congregate, canine cough will likely be spread among them. Intranasal vaccination with *Bordetella* and parainfluenza is the best safeguard, but the duration of immunity does not appear to be very long, typically a year at most. These are non-core vaccines, but vaccination is sometimes mandated by boarding kennels, obedience classes, dog shows and other places where dogs congregate to try to minimize spread of infection.

Leptospirosis: A potentially fatal disease that is more common in some geographic regions. It is capable of being spread to humans. The disease varies with the individual "serovar," or strain, of *Leptospira* involved. Since there does not appear to be much cross-protection between serovars, protection is only as good as the likelihood that the serovar in the vaccine is the same as the one in the pet's local environment. Problems with *Leptospira* vaccines are that protection does not last very long, side effects are not uncommon and a large percentage of dogs (perhaps 30%) may not respond to vaccination.

Borrelia burgdorferi: The cause of Lyme disease, the risk of which varies with the geographic area in which the pet lives and travels. Lyme disease is spread by deer ticks in the eastern US and western black-legged ticks in the western part of the country, and the risk of exposure is high in some regions. Lameness, fever and inappetence are most commonly seen in affected dogs. The extent of protection from the vaccine has not been conclusively demonstrated.

Coronavirus: This disease has a high risk of exposure, especially in areas where dogs congregate, but it typically causes only mild to moderate digestive upset (diarrhea, vomiting, etc.). Vaccines are available, but the duration of protection is believed to be relatively short and the effectiveness of the vaccine in preventing infection is considered low.

There are many other vaccinations available, including those for *Giardia* and canine adenovirus-1. While there may be some specific indications for their use, and local risk factors to be considered, they are not widely recommended for most dogs.

fluenza, *Bordetella bronchiseptica*, leptospirosis, coronavirus and borreliosis (Lyme disease) are considered non-core needs and best reserved for

> ### HIT ME WITH A HOT SPOT
> What is a hot spot? Technically known as pyotraumatic dermatitis, a hot spot is an infection on the dog's coat, usually by the rear end, under the tail or on a leg, which the dog inflicts upon himself. The dog licks and bites the itchy spot until it becomes inflamed and infected. The hot spot can range in size from the circumference of a grape to the circumference of an apple. Provided that the hot spot is not related to a deeper bacterial infection, it can be treated topically by clipping the area, cleaning the sore and giving prednisone. For bacterial infections, antibiotics are required. In some cases, an Elizabethan collar is required to keep the dog from further irritating the hot spot. The itching can intensify and the pain becomes worse. Medicated shampoos and cool compresses, drying agents and topical steroids may be prescribed by your vet as well.
>
> Hot spots can be caused by fleas, an allergy, an ear infection, anal sac problems, mange or a foreign irritant. Likewise, they can be linked to psychoses. The underlying problem must be addressed in addition to the hot spot itself.

animals that demonstrate reasonable risk of contracting the diseases.

NEUTERING/SPAYING
Sterilization procedures (neutering for males/spaying for females) are meant to accomplish several purposes. While the underlying premise is to address the risk of pet overpopulation, there are also some medical and behavioral benefits to the surgeries as well. For females, spaying prior to the first estrus (heat cycle) leads to a marked reduction in the risk of mammary cancer and other serious female problems. There also will be no manifestations of "heat" to attract male dogs and no bleeding in the house. For males, there is prevention of testicular cancer and a reduction in the risk

Gordons love their time outside! Be diligent with skin and coat checks to make sure that your dog isn't harboring debris, insects or other irritants picked up outdoors.

diminishing of urine marking, roaming and mounting.

While neutering and spaying do indeed prevent animals from contributing to pet overpopulation, even no-cost and low-cost neutering options have not eliminated the problem. Perhaps one of the main reasons for this is that individuals that intentionally breed their dogs and those that allow their animals to run at large are the main causes of unwanted offspring. Also, animals in shelters are often there because they were abandoned or relinquished, not because they came from unplanned matings. Neutering/spaying is important, but it

Food allergies may not be immediately evident. Keep track of what you feed your dog at all stages of life so that you will be better prepared to identify possible allergens if problems occur.

of prostate problems. In both sexes there may be some limited reduction in aggressive behaviors toward other dogs, and some

FOOD ALLERGY

Severe itching, leading to bald patches and open sores on the feet, face, ears, armpits and groin, could be caused by a food allergy. Studies indicate that up to 10% of dogs suffer from food allergies, which develop slowly over time without a change in diet. Dogs who suffer from chronic ear problems may actually have a food allergy. Unfortunately, there are no tests available to determine whether your dog definitely suffers from a food allergy. The dog will be miserable and you will be frustrated and stressed.

Take the problem into your own hands and kitchen. Select a type of meat that your dog is not getting from his existing diet, perhaps white fish, lamb or venison, and prepare a home-cooked food. The food should consist of two parts carbohydrate (rice, pasta or potatoes) and one part protein (the chosen meat). It's better not to start with soy as the protein source unless all of the meats cause a reaction.

Monitor your dog's intake carefully. He must eat only your prepared meal without any treats or side-trips to the garbage can. All family members (and visiting friends) must be informed of the plan. After four or five weeks on the new diet, you will reintroduce a portion of his original diet to determine whether this food is the cause of the allergic reactions. Once the dog reacts to the change in diet, resume the new diet. Make dietary modifications every two weeks and keep careful records of any reactions the dog has to the diet.

should be considered in the context of the real causes of animals' ending up in shelters and eventually being euthanized.

In males, neutering has traditionally referred to castration, which involves the surgical removal of both testicles. While still a significant piece of surgery, there is not the abdominal exposure that is required in the female surgery. In addition, there is now a chemical sterilization option, in which a solution is injected into each testicle, leading to atrophy of the sperm-producing cells. This can typically be done under sedation rather than full anesthesia. This is a relatively new approach, and there are no long-term clinical studies yet available.

Neutering/spaying is typically done around six months of age at most veterinary hospitals, although techniques have been pioneered to perform the procedures in animals as young as eight weeks of age. In general, the surgeries on the very young animals are done for the specific reason of sterilizing them before they go to their new homes. This is done in some shelter hospitals for assurance that the animals will definitely not produce any pups. Otherwise, these organizations need to rely on owners to comply with their wishes to have the animals "altered" at a later date, something that does not always happen.

There are some exciting immunocontraceptive "vaccines" currently under development, and there may be a time when contraception in pets will not require surgical procedures. We anxiously await these developments.

WHIPWORMS

In North America, whipworms are counted among the most common parasitic worms in dogs. The scientific name of the whipworm that most commonly attacks dogs is *Trichuris vulpis*. These worms attach themselves in the lower parts of the intestine, where they feed. Affected dogs may experience only upset tummies, colic and diarrhea. These worms, however, can live for months or years in the dog, beginning their larval stage in the small intestine, spending their adult stage in the large intestine and finally passing infective eggs through the dog's feces. The only way to detect whipworms is through a fecal examination, though this is not always foolproof. Treatment for whipworms is tricky, due to the worms' unusual life-cycle pattern; very often dogs are reinfected caused by exposure to infective eggs on the ground. The whipworm eggs can survive in the environment for as long as five years; thus, cleaning up droppings in your own back yard as well as in public places is absolutely essential for sanitation purposes and the health of your dog and others.

S. E. M. by Dr. Dennis Kunkel, University of Hawaii

A scanning electron micrograph of a dog flea, Ctenocephalides canis, on dog hair.

EXTERNAL PARASITES

FLEAS

Fleas have been around for millions of years and, while we have better tools now for controlling them than at any time in the past, there still is little chance that they will end up on an endangered species list. Actually, they are very well adapted to living on our pets, and they continue to adapt as we make advances.

The female flea can consume 15 times her weight in blood during active reproduction and can lay as many as 40 eggs a day. These eggs are very resistant to the effects of insecticides. They hatch into larvae, which then mature and spin cocoons. The immature fleas reside in this pupal stage until the time is right for feeding. This pupal stage is also very resistant to the effects of insecticides, and pupae can last in the environment without feeding for many months. Newly emergent fleas are attracted to animals by the warmth of the animals' bodies, movement and exhaled carbon dioxide. However, when they first emerge from their cocoons, they orient towards light; thus when an animal passes between a flea and the light source, casting a shadow, the flea pounces and starts to feed. If the animal turns out to be a dog or cat, the reproductive cycle continues. If the flea lands on another type of animal, including a person, the flea will bite but will then look for a more appropriate host. An emerging adult flea can survive without feeding for up to 12 months but, once it tastes blood, it can survive off its host for only 3 to 4 days.

It was once thought that fleas spend most of their lives in the environment, but we now know that fleas won't willingly jump off a dog unless leaping to another dog or when physically removed by brushing, bathing or other manipulation. Flea eggs, on the other hand, are shiny and smooth, and they roll off the animal and into the environment. The eggs, larvae and pupae then exist in the environment, but once the adult finds a susceptible animal, it's home sweet home until the flea is forced to seek refuge elsewhere.

Since adult fleas live on the animal and immature forms survive in the environment, a successful treatment plan must address all stages of the flea life cycle. There are now several safe and effective flea-control products that can be applied on a monthly

> ### FLEA PREVENTION FOR YOUR DOG
> - Discuss with your veterinarian the safest product to protect your dog, likely in the form of a monthly tablet or a liquid preparation placed on the back of the dog's neck.
> - For dogs suffering from flea-bite dermatitis, a shampoo or topical insecticide treatment is required.
> - Your lawn and property should be sprayed with an insecticide designed to kill fleas and ticks that lurk outdoors.
> - Using a flea comb, check the dog's coat regularly for any signs of parasites.
> - Practice good housekeeping. Vacuum floors, carpets and furniture regularly, especially in the areas that the dog frequents, and wash the dog's bedding weekly.
> - Follow up house-cleaning with carpet shampoos and sprays to rid the house of fleas at all stages of development. Insect growth regulators are the safest option.

basis. These include fipronil, imidacloprid, selamectin and permethrin (found in several formulations). Most of these products have significant flea-killing rates within 24 hours. However, none of them will control the immature forms in the environment. To accomplish this, there are a variety of insect growth regulators that can be sprayed into

THE FLEA'S LIFE CYCLE

What came first, the flea or the egg? This age-old mystery is more difficult to comprehend than the actual cycle of the flea. Fleas usually live only about four months. A female can lay 2,000 eggs in her lifetime.

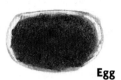

PHOTO BY CAROLINA BIOLOGICAL SUPPLY CO.

Egg

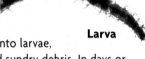

PHOTO BY CAROLINA BIOLOGICAL SUPPLY CO.

Larva

After ten days of rolling around your carpet or under your furniture, the eggs hatch into larvae, which feed on various and sundry debris. In days or months, depending on the climate, the larvae spin cocoons and develop into the pupal or nymph stage, which quickly develop into fleas.

Pupa

These immature fleas must locate a host within 10 to 14 days or they will die. Only about 1% of the flea population exist as adult fleas, while the other 99% exist as eggs, larvae or pupae.

KILL FLEAS THE NATURAL WAY

If you choose not to go the route of conventional medication, there are some natural ways to ward off fleas:

• Dust your dog with a natural flea powder, composed of such herbal goodies as rosemary, wormwood, pennyroyal, citronella, rue, tobacco powder and eucalyptus.

• Apply diatomaceous earth, the fossilized remains of single-cell algae, to your carpets, furniture and pet's bedding. Even though it's not good for dogs, it's even worse for fleas, which will dry up swiftly and die.

• Brush your dog frequently, give him adequate exercise and let him fast occasionally. All of these activities strengthen the dog's immune system and make him more resistant to disease and parasites.

• Bathe your dog with a capful of pennyroyal or eucalyptus oil.

• Feed a natural diet, free of additives and preservatives. Add some fresh garlic and brewer's yeast to the dog's morning portion, as these items have flea-repelling properties.

the environment (e.g., pyriprox-yfen, methoprene, fenoxycarb) as well as insect development inhibitors such as lufenuron that can be administered. These compounds have no effect on adult fleas, but they stop immature forms from developing into

adults. In years gone by, we relied heavily on toxic insecticides (such as organophosphates, organochlo-rines and carbamates) to manage the flea problem, but today's options are not only much safer to use on our pets but also safer for the environment.

TICKS

Ticks are members of the spider class (arachnids) and are blood-sucking parasites capable of transmitting a variety of diseases, including Lyme disease, ehrlichiosis, babesiosis and Rocky Mountain spotted fever. It's easy to see ticks on your own skin, but it is more of a challenge when your furry companion is affected. Whenever you happen to be planning a stroll in a tick-infested area (especially forests, grassy or wooded areas or parks) be prepared to do a thorough inspection of your dog afterward to search for ticks. Ticks can be tricky, so make sure you spend time looking in the ears, between the toes and everywhere else where a tick might hide. Ticks need to be attached for 24–72 hours before they transmit most of the diseases that they carry, so you do have a window of opportunity for some preventive intervention.

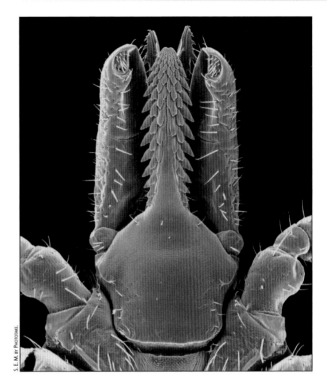

S. E. M. BY PHOTOTAKE.

A scanning electron micrograph of the head of a female deer tick, *Ixodes dammini*, a parasitic tick that carries Lyme disease.

A TICKING BOMB

There is nothing good about a tick's harpooning his nose into your dog's skin. Among the diseases caused by ticks are Rocky Mountain spotted fever, canine ehrlichiosis, canine babesiosis, canine hepatozoonosis and Lyme disease. If a dog is allergic to the saliva of a female wood tick, he can develop tick paralysis.

Female ticks live to eat and breed. They can lay between 4,000 and 5,000 eggs and they die soon after. Males, on the other hand, live only to mate with the females and continue the process as long as they are able. Most ticks live on multiple hosts before parasitizing dogs. The immature forms typically reside on grass and shrubs, waiting for susceptible animals to walk by. The larvae and nymph stages typically feed on wildlife.

If only a few ticks are present on a dog, they can be plucked out, but it is important to remove the entire head and mouthparts,

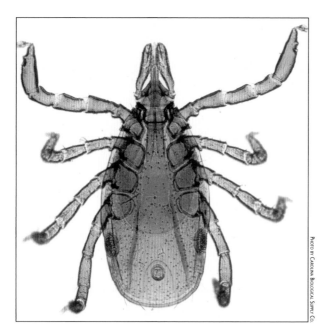

PHOTO BY CAROLINA BIOLOGICAL SUPPLY CO.

Deer tick,
Ixodes dammini.

of in a container of alcohol or household bleach.

Some of the newer flea products, specifically those with fipronil, selamectin and permethrin, have effect against some, but not all, species of tick. Flea collars containing appropriate pesticides (e.g., propoxur, chlorfenvinphos) can aid in tick control. In most areas, such collars should be placed on animals in March, at the beginning of the tick season, and changed regularly. Leaving the collar on when the pesticide level is waning invites the development of resistance. Amitraz collars are also good for tick control, and the active ingredient does not interfere with other flea-control products. The ingredient helps prevent the attachment of ticks to the skin and will cause those ticks already on the skin to detach themselves.

which may be deeply embedded in the skin. This is best accomplished with forceps designed especially for this purpose; fingers can be used but should be protected with rubber gloves, plastic wrap or at least a paper towel. The tick should be grasped as closely as possible to the animal's skin and should be pulled upward with steady, even pressure. Do not squeeze, crush or puncture the body of the tick or you risk exposure to any disease carried by that tick. Once the ticks have been removed, the sites of attachment should be disinfected. Your hands should then be washed with soap and water to further minimize risk of contagion. The tick should be disposed

TICK CONTROL

Removal of underbrush and leaf litter and the thinning of trees in areas where tick control is desired are recommended. These actions remove the cover and food sources for small animals that serve as hosts for ticks. With continued mowing of grasses in these areas, the probability of ticks' surviving is further reduced. A variety of insecticide ingredients (e.g., resmethrin, carbaryl, permethrin, chlorpyrifos, dioxathion and allethrin) are registered for tick control around the home.

MITES

Mites are tiny arachnid parasites that parasitize the skin of dogs. Skin diseases caused by mites are referred to as "mange," and there are many different forms seen in dogs. These forms are very different from one another, each one warranting an individual description.

Sarcoptic mange, or scabies, is one of the itchiest conditions that affects dogs. The microscopic *Sarcoptes* mites burrow into the superficial layers of the skin and can drive dogs crazy with itchiness. They are also communicable to people, although they can't complete their reproductive cycle on people. In addition to being tiny, the mites also are often difficult to find when trying to make a diagnosis. Skin scrapings from multiple areas are examined microscopically but, even then, sometimes the mites cannot be found.

Fortunately, scabies is relatively easy to treat, and there are a variety of products that will successfully kill the mites. Since the mites can't live in the environment for very long without feeding, a complete cure is usually possible within four to eight weeks.

Cheyletiellosis is caused by a relatively large mite, which sometimes can be seen even without a microscope. Often referred to as "walking dandruff," this also causes itching, but not usually as profound as with scabies. While *Cheyletiella* mites can survive somewhat longer

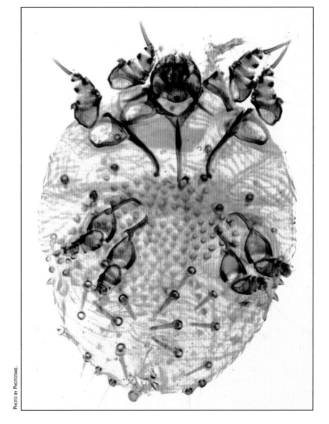

PHOTO BY PHOTOTAKE.

in the environment than scabies mites, they too are relatively easy to treat, being responsive to not only the medications used to treat scabies but also often to flea-control products.

Otodectes cynotis is the canine ear mite and is one of the more common causes of mange, especially in young dogs in shelters or pet stores. That's because the mites are typically present in large numbers and are quickly spread to nearby animals. The mites rarely do much harm but

Sarcoptes scabiei, commonly known as the "itch mite."

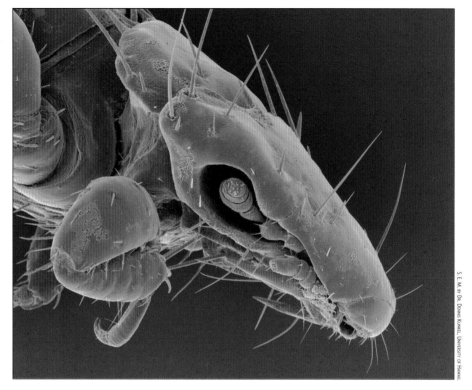

S. E. M. BY DR. DENNIS KUNKEL, UNIVERSITY OF HAWAII.

Micrograph of a dog louse, *Heterodoxus spiniger*. Female lice attach their eggs to the hairs of the dog. As the eggs hatch, the larval lice bite and feed on the blood. Lice can also feed on dead skin and hair. This feeding activity can cause hair loss and skin problems.

can be difficult to eradicate if the treatment regimen is not comprehensive. While many try to treat the condition with ear drops only, this is the most common cause of treatment failure. Ear drops cause the mites to simply move out of the ears and as far away as possible (usually to the base of the tail) until the insecticide levels in the ears drop to an acceptable level— then it's back to business as usual! The successful treatment of ear mites requires treating all animals in the household with a systemic insecticide, such as selamectin, or a combination of miticidal ear drops combined with whole-body flea-control preparations.

Demodicosis, sometimes referred to as red mange, can be one of the most difficult forms of mange to treat. Part of the problem has to do with the fact that the mites live in the hair follicles and they are relatively well shielded from topical and systemic products. The main issue, however, is that demodectic mange typically results only when there is some underlying process interfering with the dog's immune system.

Since *Demodex* mites are normal residents of the skin of

mammals, including humans, there is usually a mite population explosion only when the immune system fails to keep the number of mites in check. In young animals, the immune deficit may be transient or may reflect an actual inherited immune problem. In older animals, demodicosis is usually seen only when there is another disease hampering the immune system, such as diabetes, cancer, thyroid problems or the use of immune-suppressing drugs. Accordingly, treatment involves not only trying to kill the mange mites but also discerning what is interfering with immune function and correcting it if possible.

Chiggers represent several different species of mite that don't parasitize dogs specifically, but do latch on to passersby and can cause irritation. The problem is most prevalent in wooded areas in the late summer and fall. Treatment is not difficult, as the mites do not complete their life cycle on dogs and are susceptible to a variety of miticidal products.

MOSQUITOES

Mosquitoes have long been known to transmit a variety of diseases to people, as well as just being biting pests during warm weather. They also pose a real risk to pets. Not only do they carry deadly heartworms but

recently there also has been much concern over their involvement with West Nile virus. While we can avoid heartworm with the use of preventive medications, there are no such preventives for West Nile virus. The only method of prevention in endemic areas is active mosquito control. Fortunately, most dogs that have been exposed to the virus only developed flu-like symptoms and, to date, there have not been the large number of reported deaths in canines as seen in some other species.

Illustration of *Demodex folliculoram.*

MOSQUITO REPELLENT

Low concentrations of DEET (less than 10%), found in many human mosquito repellents, have been safely used in dogs but, in these concentrations, probably give only about two hours of protection. DEET may be safe in these small concentrations, but since it is not licensed for use on dogs, there is no research proving its safety for dogs. Products containing permethrin give the longest-lasting protection, perhaps two to four weeks. As DEET is not licensed for use on dogs, and both DEET and permethrin can be quite toxic to cats, appropriate care should be exercised. Other products, such as those containing oil of citronella, also have some mosquito-repellent activity, but typically have a relatively short duration of action.

S. E. M. BY DR. DENNIS KUNKEL, UNIVERSITY OF HAWAII. INSET BY TAM C. NGUYEN.

ASCARID DANGERS

The most commonly encountered worms in dogs are roundworms known as ascarids. *Toxascaris leonine* and *Toxocara canis* are the two species that infect dogs. Subsisting in the dog's stomach and intestines, adult roundworms can grow to 7 inches in length and adult females can lay in excess of 200,000 eggs in a single day.

In humans, visceral larval migrans affects people who have ingested eggs of *Toxocara canis*, which frequently contaminates children's sandboxes, beaches and park grounds. The roundworms reside in the human's stomach and intestines, as they would in a dog's, but do not mature. Instead, they find their way to the liver, lungs and skin, or even to the heart or kidneys in severe cases. Deworming puppies is critical in preventing the infection in humans, and young children should never handle nursing pups who have not been dewormed.

The ascarid roundworm *Toxocara canis*, showing the mouth with three lips. INSET: Photomicrograph of the roundworm *Ascaris lumbricoides*.

INTERNAL PARASITES: WORMS

ASCARIDS

Ascarids are intestinal roundworms that rarely cause severe disease in dogs. Nonetheless, they are of major public health significance because they can be transferred to people. Sadly, it is children who are most commonly affected by the parasite, probably from inadvertently ingesting ascarid-contaminated soil. In fact, many yards and children's sand-boxes contain appreciable numbers of ascarid eggs. So, while ascarids don't bite dogs or latch onto their intestines to suck blood, they do cause some nasty medical conditions in children and are best eradicated from our furry friends. Because pups can start passing ascarid eggs by three weeks of age, most parasite-control programs begin at two weeks of age and are repeated every two weeks until pups are eight weeks old. It is important to

HOOKED ON ANCYLOSTOMA

Adult dogs can become infected by the bloodsucking nematodes we commonly call hookworms via ingesting larvae from the ground or via the larvae penetrating the dog's skin. It is not uncommon for infected dogs to show no symptoms of hookworm infestation. Sometimes symptoms occur within ten days of exposure. These symptoms can include bloody diarrhea, anemia, loss of weight and general weakness. Dogs pass the hookworm eggs in their stools, which serves as the vet's method of identifying the infestation. The hookworm larvae can encyst themselves in the dog's tissues and be released when the dog is experiencing stress.

Caused by an *Ancylostoma* species whose common host is the dog, cutaneous larval migrans affects humans, causing itching and lumps and streaks beneath the surface of the skin.

S. E. M. BY DR. DENNIS KUNKEL, UNIVERSITY OF HAWAII.

realize that bitches can pass ascarids to their pups even if they test negative prior to whelping. Accordingly, bitches are best treated at the same time as the pups.

HOOKWORMS

Unlike ascarids, hookworms do latch onto a dog's intestinal tract and can cause significant loss of blood and protein. Similar to ascarids, hookworms can be transmitted to humans, where they cause a condition known as cutaneous larval migrans. Dogs can become infected either by consuming the infective larvae or by the larvae's penetrating the skin directly. People most often get infected when they are lying on the ground (such as on a beach) and the larvae penetrate the skin. Yes, the larvae can penetrate through a beach blanket. Hookworms are typically susceptible to the same medications used to treat ascarids.

The hookworm *Ancylostoma caninum* infests the intestines of dogs. INSET: Note the row of hooks at the posterior end, used to anchor the worm to the intestinal wall.

WHIPWORMS

Whipworms latch onto the lower aspects of the dog's colon and can cause cramping and diarrhea. Eggs do not start to appear in the dog's feces until about three months after the dog was infected. This worm has a peculiar life cycle, which makes it more difficult to control than ascarids or hook-worms. The good thing is that whipworms rarely are transferred to people.

Some of the medications used to treat ascarids and hookworms are also effective against whipworms, but, in general, a separate treatment protocol is needed. Since most of the medications are effective against the adults but not the eggs or larvae, treatment is typically repeated in three weeks, and then often in three

Adult whipworm, *Trichuris* sp., an intestinal parasite.

S. E. M. BY DR. DENNIS KUNKEL, UNIVERSITY OF HAWAII.

WORM-CONTROL GUIDELINES

- Practice sanitary habits with your dog and home.
- Clean up after your dog and don't let him sniff or eat other dogs' droppings.
- Control insects and fleas in the dog's environment. Fleas, lice, cockroaches, beetles, mice and rats can act as hosts for various worms.
- Prevent dogs from eating uncooked meat, raw poultry and dead animals.
- Keep dogs and children from playing in sand and soil.
- Kennel dogs on cement or gravel; avoid dirt runs.
- Administer heartworm preventives regularly.
- Have your vet examine your dog's stools at your annual visits.
- Select a boarding kennel carefully so as to avoid contamination from other dogs or an unsanitary environment.
- Prevent dogs from roaming. Obey local leash laws.

months as well. Unfortunately, since dogs don't develop resistance to whipworms, it is difficult to prevent them from getting rein-fected if they visit soil contami-nated with whipworm eggs.

TAPEWORMS

There are many different species of tapeworm that affect dogs, but *Dipylidium caninum* is probably the most common and is spread by fleas. Flea larvae feed on organic debris and tapeworm eggs in the environment and, when a dog chews at himself and manages to ingest fleas, he might get a dose of tapeworm at the same time. The tapeworm then develops further in the intestine of the dog.

The tapeworm itself, which is a parasitic flatworm that latches onto the intestinal wall, is composed of numerous segments. When the segments break off into the intestine (as proglottids), they may accumulate around the rectum, like grains of rice. While this tapeworm is disgusting in its behavior, it is not directly communicable to humans (although humans can also get infected by swallowing fleas).

A much more dangerous flatworm is *Echinococcus multilocularis*, which is typically found in foxes, coyotes and wolves. The eggs are passed in the feces and infect rodents, and, when dogs eat the rodents, the dogs can be infected by thousands of adult tapeworms. While the parasites don't cause many problems in dogs, this is considered the most lethal worm infection that people can get. Take appropriate precautions if you live in an area in which these tapeworms are found. Do not use mulch that may contain feces of dogs, cats or wildlife, and discourage your pets from hunting

wildlife. Treat these tapeworm infections aggressively in pets, because if humans get infected, approximately half die.

HEARTWORMS

Heartworm disease is caused by the parasite *Dirofilaria immitis* and is seen in dogs around the world. A member of the roundworm group, it is spread between dogs by the bite of an infected mosquito. The mosquito injects infective larvae into the dog's skin with its bite, and these larvae develop under the skin for a period of time before making their way to the heart. There they develop into adults, which grow and create blockages of the heart, lungs and major blood vessels there. They also start producing offspring (microfilariae)

A dog tapeworm proglottid (body segment).

The dog tapeworm *Taenia pisiformis*.

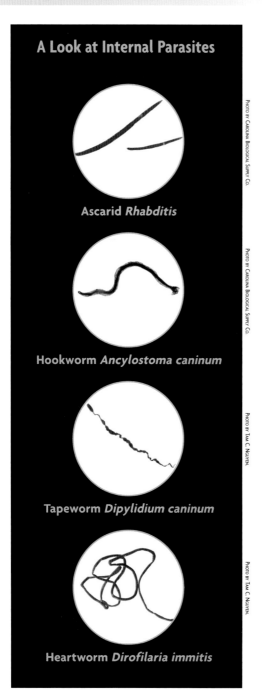

A Look at Internal Parasites

Ascarid *Rhabditis*

Hookworm *Ancylostoma caninum*

Tapeworm *Dipylidium caninum*

Heartworm *Dirofilaria immitis*

Photo by Carolina Biological Supply Co.

Photo by Carolina Biological Supply Co.

Photo by Tam C. Nguyen

Photo by Tam C. Nguyen

and these microfilariae circulate in the bloodstream, waiting to hitch a ride when the next mosquito bites. Once in the mosquito, the microfilariae develop into infective larvae and the entire process is repeated.

When dogs get infected with heartworm, over time they tend to develop symptoms associated with heart disease, such as coughing, exercise intolerance and potentially many other manifestations. Diagnosis is confirmed by either seeing the microfilariae themselves in blood samples or using immunologic tests (antigen testing) to identify the presence of adult heartworms. Since antigen tests measure the presence of adult heartworms and microfilarial tests measure offspring produced by adults, neither are positive until six to seven months after the initial infection. However, the beginning of damage can occur by fifth-stage larvae as early as three months after infection. Thus it is possible for dogs to be harboring problem-causing larvae for up to three months before either type of test would identify an infection.

The good news is that there are great protocols available for preventing heartworm in dogs. Testing is critical in the process, and it is important to understand the benefits as well as the limitations of such testing. All dogs six months of age or older that have not been on continuous heartworm-preventive medication should be

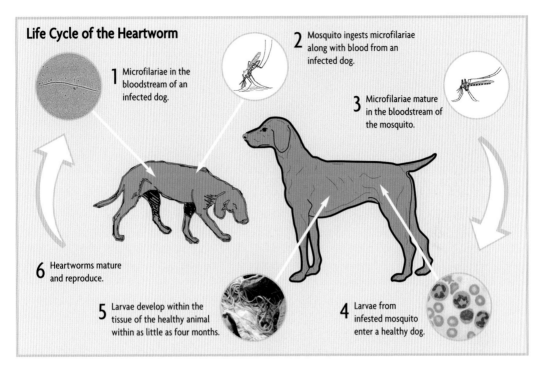

Life Cycle of the Heartworm

1 Microfilariae in the bloodstream of an infected dog.

2 Mosquito ingests microfilariae along with blood from an infected dog.

3 Microfilariae mature in the bloodstream of the mosquito.

4 Larvae from infested mosquito enter a healthy dog.

5 Larvae develop within the tissue of the healthy animal within as little as four months.

6 Heartworms mature and reproduce.

screened with microfilarial or antigen tests. For dogs receiving preventive medication, periodic antigen testing helps assess the effectiveness of the preventives. The American Heartworm Society guidelines suggest that annual retesting may not be necessary when owners have absolutely provided continuous heartworm prevention. Retesting on a two- to three-year interval may be sufficient in these cases. However, your veterinarian will likely have specific guidelines under which heartworm preventives will be prescribed, and many prefer to err on the side of safety and retest annually.

It is indeed fortunate that heartworm is relatively easy to prevent because treatments can be as life-threatening as the disease itself. Treatment requires a two-step process that kills the adult heartworms first and then the microfilariae. Prevention is obviously preferable; this involves a once-monthly oral or topical treatment. The most common oral preventives include ivermectin (not suitable for some breeds), moxidectin and milbemycin oxime; the once-a-month topical drug selamectin provides heartworm protection in addition to flea, some types of tick and other parasite controls.

GORDON SETTER

When we bring home a puppy, full of the energy and exuberance that accompanies youth, we hope for a long, happy and fulfilling relationship with the new family member. Even when we adopt an older dog, we look forward to the years of companionship ahead with a new canine friend. However, aging is inevitable for all creatures, and there will come a time when your Gordon Setter reaches his senior years and will need special considerations and attention to his care.

WHEN IS MY DOG A "SENIOR"?
In general, purebred dogs are considered to have achieved senior status when they reach 75% of their breed's average lifespan, with lifespan being based on breed size along with other factors. Your Gordon Setter has an average lifespan of about 10–12 years and thus is a senior citizen at around 7 years old.

Obviously, the old "seven dog years to one human year" theory is not exact. In puppyhood, a

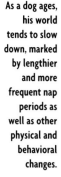

As a dog ages, his world tends to slow down, marked by lengthier and more frequent nap periods as well as other physical and behavioral changes.

dog's year is actually comparable to more than seven human years, considering the puppy's rapid growth during his first year. Then, in adulthood, the ratio decreases. Regardless, the more viable rule of thumb is that the larger the dog, the shorter his expected lifespan. Of course, this can vary among individual dogs, with many living longer than expected, which we hope is the case. Gordons have lived to age 14 and older!

WHAT ARE THE SIGNS OF AGING?

By the time your dog has reached his senior years, you will know him very well, so the physical and behavioral changes that accompany aging should be noticeable to you. Humans and dogs share the most obvious physical sign of aging: gray hair! Graying often occurs first on the muzzle and face, around the eyes. Other telltale signs are the dog's overall decrease in activity. Your older dog might be more content to nap and rest, and he may not show the same old enthusiasm when it's time to play in the yard or go for a walk. Other physical signs include significant weight loss or gain; more labored movement; skin and coat problems, possibly hair loss; sight and/or hearing problems; changes in toileting habits, perhaps seeming "unhousebroken" at times; tooth decay, bad breath or other mouth problems.

WEATHER WORRIES
Older pets are less tolerant of extremes in weather, both heat and cold. Your older dog should not spend extended periods in the sun; when outdoors in the warm weather, make sure he does not become overheated. In chilly weather, consider a sweater for your dog when outdoors and limit time spent outside. Whether or not his coat is thinning, he will need provisions to keep him warm when the weather is cold. You may even place his bed by a heating duct in your living room or bedroom.

There are behavioral changes that go along with aging, too. There are numerous causes for behavioral changes. Sometimes a dog's apparent confusion results from a physical change like diminished sight or hearing. If his confusion causes him to be afraid, he may act aggressively or defensively. He may sleep more frequently because his daily walks, though shorter now, tire him out. He may begin to experience separation anxiety or, conversely, become less interested in petting and attention.

There also are clinical conditions that cause behavioral changes in older dogs. One such condition is known as canine cognitive dysfunction (familiarly known as "old-dog" syndrome). It can be frustrating for an owner

ADAPTING TO AGE

As dogs age and their once-keen senses begin to deteriorate, they can experience stress and confusion. However, dogs are very adaptable, and most can adjust to deficiencies in their sight and hearing. As these processes often deteriorate gradually, the dog makes adjustments gradually, too. Because dogs become so familiar with the layout of their homes and yards, and with their daily routines, they are able to get around even if they cannot see or hear as well. Help your senior dog by keeping things consistent around the house. Keep up with your regular times for walking and potty trips, and do not relocate his crate or rearrange the furniture. Your dog is a very adaptable creature and can make compensation for his diminished ability, but you want to help him along the way and not make changes that will cause him confusion.

will begin to show aggressive or possessive tendencies or, conversely, a hyperactive dog will start to "mellow out."

Disease also can be the cause of behavioral changes in senior dogs. Hormonal problems (Cushing's disease is common in older dogs), diabetes and thyroid disease can cause increased appetite, which can lead to aggression related to food guarding. It's better to be proactive with your senior dog, making more frequent trips to the vet if necessary and having bloodwork done to test for the diseases that can commonly befall older dogs.

This is not to say that, as dogs age, they all fall apart physically and become nasty in personality. The aforementioned changes are discussed to alert owners to the things that may happen as their dogs get older. Many hardy dogs remain active and alert well into old age. However, it can be frustrating and heartbreaking for owners to see their beloved dogs change physically and temperamentally. Just know that it's the same Gordon Setter under there, and that he still loves you and appreciates your care, which he needs now more than ever.

whose dog is affected with cognitive dysfunction, as it can result in behavioral changes of all types, most seemingly unexplainable. Common changes include the dog's forgetting aspects of the daily routine, such as times to eat, go out for walks, relieve himself and the like. Along the same lines, you may take your dog out at the regular time for a potty trip and he may have no idea why he is there. Sometimes a placid dog

HOW DO I CARE FOR MY AGING DOG?

Again, every dog is an individual in terms of aging. Your dog might reach the estimated "senior" age for his breed and show no signs of slowing down. However, even if he shows no outward signs of aging, he should begin a senior-care program once he reaches the determined age or when advised by your vet. He may not show it, but he's not a pup anymore! By providing him with extra attention to his veterinary care at this age, you will be practicing good preventive medicine, ensuring that the rest of your dog's life will be as long, active, happy and healthy as possible. If you do notice indications of aging, such as graying and/or changes in sleeping, eating or toileting habits, this is a sign to set up a senior-care visit with your vet right away to make sure that these changes are not related to any health problems.

To start, senior dogs should visit the vet twice yearly for exams, routine tests and overall evaluations. Many veterinarians

AH, MY ACHING BONES!

As your pet ages and things that once were routine become difficult for him to handle, you may need to make some adjustments around the home to make things easier for your dog. Senior dogs affected by arthritis may have trouble moving about. If you notice this in your dog, you may have to limit him to one floor of the house so that he does not have to deal with stairs. If there are a few steps leading out into the yard, a ramp may help the dog. Likewise, he may need a ramp or a boost to get in and out of the car. Ensure that he has plenty of soft bedding on which to sleep and rest, as this will be comfortable for his aching joints. Also ensure that surfaces on which the dog walks are not slippery.

Investigate new dietary supplements made for arthritic dogs. Studies have found that products containing glucosamine added once or twice daily to the senior dog's food can have beneficial effects on the dog's joints. Many of these products also contain natural anti-inflammatories such as chondroitin, MSM and cetyl myristoleate, as well as natural herbal remedies and nutmeg. Talk to your vet about these supplements before giving them to your dog.

A good remedy for an aching dog is to give him a gentle massage each day, or even a few times a day if possible. This can be especially beneficial before your dog gets out of his bed in the morning. Just as in humans, massage can decrease pain in dogs, whether the dog is arthritic or just afflicted by the stiffness that accompanies old age. Gently massage his joints and limbs, as well as petting him on his entire body. This can help his circulation and flexibility and ease any joint or muscle aches. Massaging your dog has benefits for you, too; in fact, just petting our dogs can cause reduced levels of stress and lower our blood pressure. Massage and petting also help you find any previously undetected lumps, bumps or abnormalities. Often these are not visible and only turn up by being felt.

GDV IN OLDER DOGS
We know that bloat, or gastric dilatation-volvulus (GDV), commonly affects deep-chested dogs of all ages. Studies indicate that dogs who are over seven years of age are twice as prone to the condition as dogs half their age. Be extra-diligent about practicing the daily bloat preventives that you always should have been incorporating into your Gordon's routine.

that you feed. This information, along with his evaluation of the dog's overall condition, will enable him to suggest proper dietary changes, if needed.

This may seem like quite a work-up for your pet, but veterinarians advise that older dogs need more frequent attention so that any health problems can be detected as early as possible. Serious conditions like kidney disease, heart disease and cancer may not present outward symptoms, or the problem may go undetected if the symptoms are mistaken by owners as just part of the aging process.

There are some conditions more common in elderly dogs that are difficult to ignore. Cognitive dysfunction shares much in common with senility and Alzheimer's disease, and dogs are not immune. Dogs can become confused and/or disoriented, lose their house-training, have abnormal sleep-wake cycles and interact differently with their owners. Be heartened by the fact that, in some ways, there are more treatment options for dogs with cognitive dysfunction than for people with similar conditions. There is good evidence that continued stimulation in the form of games, play, training and exercise can help to maintain cognitive function. There are also medications (such as seligiline) and antioxidant-fortified senior diets that have been shown to be beneficial.

have special screening programs especially for senior dogs that can include a thorough physical exam; blood test to determine complete blood count; serum biochemistry test, which screens for liver, kidney and blood problems as well as cancer; urinalysis; and dental exams. With these tests, it can be determined whether your dog has any health problems; the results also establish a baseline for your pet against which future test results can be compared.

In addition to these tests, your vet may suggest additional testing, including an EKG, tests for glaucoma and other problems of the eye, chest x-rays, screening for tumors, blood pressure test, test for thyroid function and screening for parasites and reassessment of his preventive program. Your vet also will ask you questions about your dog's diet and activity level, what you feed and the amounts

Cancer is also a condition more common in the elderly. Almost all of the cancers seen in people are also seen in pets. While we can't control the effects of second-hand smoke, lung cancer, which is a major killer in humans, is relatively rare in dogs. If pets are getting regular physical examinations, cancers are often detected early. There are a variety of cancer therapies available today, and many pets continue to live happy lives with appropriate treatment.

Degenerative joint disease, often referred to as arthritis, is another malady common to both elderly dogs and humans. A lifetime of wear and tear on joints and running around at play eventually takes its toll and results in stiffness and difficulty in getting around. As dogs live longer and healthier lives, it is natural that they should eventually feel some of the effects of aging. Once again, if regular veterinary care has been available, your pet was not carrying extra pounds all those years and wearing those joints out before their time. If your pet was unfortunate enough to inherit hip dysplasia, osteochondritis dissecans or any of the other developmental orthopedic diseases, battling the onset of degenerative joint disease was probably a longstanding goal. In any case, there are now many effective remedies for managing degenerative joint disease and a number of remarkable surgeries as well.

Aside from the extra veterinary care, there is much you can do at home to keep your older dog in good condition. The dog's diet is an important factor. If your dog's appetite decreases, he will not be getting the nutrients he needs. He also will lose weight, which is unhealthy for a dog at a proper weight. Conversely, an older dog's metabolism is slower and he usually exercises less, but he should not be allowed to become obese. Obesity in an older dog is especially risky because extra pounds mean extra stress on the body, increasing his vulnerability to heart disease. Additionally, the extra pounds make it harder for the dog to move about.

You should discuss age-related feeding changes with your

Let your Gordon set the pace of his exercise. While accompanying you on a skate may have been enjoyed in younger days, he will let you know if it gets to be too much for him.

vet. For a dog who has lost interest in food, it may be suggested to try some different types of food until you find something new that the dog likes. For an obese dog, a "light"-formula dog food or reducing food portions may be advised, along with exercise appropriate to his physical condition and energy level.

As for exercise, the senior dog should not be allowed to become a "couch potato" despite his old age. He may not be able to handle

COPING WITH A BLIND DOG

Blindness is one of the unfortunate realities of growing old for both dogs and humans. Owners of blind dogs should not give up hope, as most dogs adapt to their compromised state with grace and patience. A sudden loss of sight poses more stress on the dog than a gradual loss, such as that through cataracts. Some dogs may need your assistance to help them get around; others will move around seemingly uninhibited. Owners may need to retrain the dog to handle some basic tasks. Teaching commands like "Wait," "Stop" and "Slow" are handy as you help the dog learn to maneuver around his world. You are now more than the team captain, you're the coach and cheerleader! If your blind dog is showing signs of depression, it is your job to encourage him and give him moral support, just as you might for a member of your family or a good friend.

the morning run, long walks and vigorous games of fetch, but he still needs to get up and get moving. Keep up with your daily walks, but keep the distances shorter and let your dog set the pace. If he gets to the point where he's not up for walks, let him stroll around the yard. On the other hand, many dogs remain very active in their senior years, so base changes to the exercise program on your own individual dog and what he's capable of. Don't worry, your Gordon Setter will let you know when it's time to rest.

Keep up with your grooming routine as you always have. Be extra-diligent about checking the skin and coat for problems. Older dogs can experience thinning coats as a normal aging process, but they can also lose hair as a result of medical problems. Some thinning is normal, but patches of baldness or the loss of significant amounts of hair is not.

Hopefully, you've been regular with brushing your dog's teeth throughout his life. Healthy teeth directly affect overall good health. We already know that bacteria from gum infections can enter the dog's body through the damaged gums and travel to the organs. At a stage in life when his organs don't function as well as they used to, you don't want anything to put additional strain on them. Clean teeth also contribute to a healthy immune system. Offering the dental-type chews in addition to toothbrushing can help, as they remove plaque and tartar as the dog chews.

Along with the same good care you've given him all of his life, pay a little extra attention to your dog in his senior years and keep up with twice-yearly trips to the vet. The sooner a problem is uncovered, the greater the chances of a full recovery.

SAYING GOODBYE

While you can help your dog live as long a life as possible, you can't help him live forever. A dog's lifespan is short when compared to that of a human, so it is inevitable that pet owners will experience loss. To many, losing a beloved dog is like losing a family member. Our dogs are part of our lives every day; they are our true loyal friends and always seem to know when it's time to comfort us, to celebrate with us or to just provide the company of a caring friend. Even when we know that our dog is nearing his final days, we can never quite prepare for his being gone.

Many dogs live out long lives and simply die of old age. Others unfortunately are taken suddenly by illness or accident, and still others find their senior years compromised by disease and physical problems. In some of these cases, owners find them-

PET LOSS AND CHILDREN

Everyone in the family will be affected by the death of a pet. Many children form strong bonds with their dogs, so losing a pet can be especially painful. For some children, losing a pet will be their first experience with the death of a loved one. This can present a difficult and awkward situation to parents, who must provide a delicate yet honest explanation appropriate to the ages of the children. Regardless of the child's age, he should be encouraged to talk about and express his feelings, and to ask questions. Providing explanations that the dog is "asleep" or has "gone away" may cause a child to think that the pet will return or that death is temporary, so euphemisms such as these may be best avoided. Children at different age levels will manifest grief in different ways. Younger children, say between two and six years of age, have less understanding of what death is, while older children, adolescents and teens grasp the concept and may manifest their grief more outwardly, possibly even experiencing denial. At any age, open discussions should be encouraged so that children can express their grief and concerns. Of course, children should be part of the decision of whether or not to get a new pet. Generally, the younger the child, the more readily he will accept a new pet into the family.

MEMORIALIZING YOUR PET

Whether and how you choose to memorialize your pet is completely up to you. Some owners feel that this helps their healing process by allowing them some closure. Likewise, some owners feel that memorialization is a meaningful way to acknowledge their departed pets. Some owners opt to bury their deceased pets in their own yards, using special stones, flowers or trees to mark the sites. Others opt for the services of a pet cemetery, in which many of the privileges available for humans, such as funeral and viewing services, caskets and gravestones, are available for pets. Cremation is an option, either individual or communal. Owners then can opt to have their dogs' ashes buried, scattered or kept in an urn as a memorial. Your vet will likely know of the services available in your locality and can help you make arrangements if you choose one of these options.

selves having to make difficult decisions.

WHAT IS EUTHANASIA?

When the end comes for a beloved pet, it is a very difficult time for the owners. This time is made even more difficult when the owners are faced with making a choice regarding euthanasia, more commonly known as having a very sick or very aged dog "put to sleep" or "put down."

Euthanasia is the term used for the act of ending the life of a pet who is suffering from a terminal illness or an incurable condition. Euthanasia is usually accomplished by injection or other medical means that do not cause pain to the patient. The most common type of veterinary euthanasia is that the pet is injected with a concentrated dose of anesthesia, causing unconsciousness within a few seconds and death soon after. This process is painless for the dog; the only discomfort he may feel is the prick of the needle, the same as he would with any other injection.

The decision of whether or not to euthanize is undoubtedly the hardest that owners have to make regarding their pets. It is a very emotional decision, yet it requires much clear thinking, discussion with the vet and, of course, discussion with all family members. During this time, owners will experience many different feelings: guilt, sadness, possibly anger at over having to make this type of decision. Many times it is hard to actually come to a decision, thinking that maybe the dog will miraculously recover or that maybe he will succumb to his illness, making the decision no longer necessary.

When faced with the decision to euthanize, you must take many things into consideration; first and foremost, what is best for your dog? Hopefully you have a good relationship with a vet whose medical opinion you trust and with whom you can discuss your decision openly and honestly. Remember that good vets are animal lovers, too, and want the best for their patients. Your vet should talk to you about your dog's condition and the reality of what the rest of his days will be like; will he be able to live out his days relatively comfortably or will the rest of his life be filled with pain? Many feel that euthanasia is the way to mercifully end a pet's suffering.

You have many factors to consider. Of course, you will speak with your vet and will involve all members of the family in each step of the decision-making process. Some of the things to think about include the current quality of your pet's life, whether he is constantly ill and/or in pain, whether there are things you can do to give him a comfortable life even if he has an incurable condition, whether you've explored all treatment problems, whether you've discussed the behavioral aspects of your pet's problems with an expert and whether you've thoroughly discussed with the vet your dog's prognosis and the likelihood of his ever again enjoying a more normal life.

Of course, the aforementioned considerations present just some of the things that you will need to think about. You will have many questions and concerns of your own. Never feel pressured; take time to make a decision with which you will be comfortable. You may want to speak with other owners who have gone through this. If you are religious, you can turn to clergy members for advice.

If you've come to the decision that euthanasia is the right choice for your pet, there are a few further, equally heartrending, choices to make. Do you or another family member want to be present with your dog during the procedure? How will you say goodbye? Should you arrange for someone to accompany you to the vet for support so that you don't have to drive in a state of grief? Again, your emotions will be running high during this very difficult time, so think your decisions through clearly and rely on the support of family and friends.

SHOWING YOUR
GORDON SETTER

Showing your Gordon can be an enjoyable and rewarding experience as you participate together, further your bond and maybe even have some success.

Is dog showing in your blood? Are you excited by the idea of gaiting your handsome Gordon Setter around the ring to the thunderous applause of an enthusiastic audience? Are you certain that your beloved Gordon Setter is flawless? You are not alone! Every loving owner thinks that his dog has no faults, or too few to mention. No matter how many times an owner reads the breed standard, he cannot find any faults in his aristocratic companion dog. If this sounds like you, and if you are considering entering your Gordon Setter in a dog show, here are some basic questions to ask yourself:

- Did you purchase a "show-quality" puppy from the breeder?
- Is your puppy at least six months of age?
- Does the puppy exhibit correct show type for his breed?
- Does your puppy have any disqualifying faults?
- Is your Gordon Setter registered with the American Kennel Club?
- How much time do you have to devote to training, grooming, conditioning and exhibiting your dog?
- Do you understand the rules and regulations of a dog show?
- Do you have time to learn how to show your dog properly?
- Do you have the financial resources to invest in showing your dog?
- Will you show the dog yourself or hire a professional handler?
- Do you have a vehicle that can accommodate your weekend trips to the dog shows?

AKC GROUPS

For showing purposes, the American Kennel Club divides its recognized breeds into seven groups: Sporting Dogs, Hounds, Working Dogs, Terriers, Toys, Non-Sporting Dogs and Herding Dogs.

FOR MORE INFORMATION...
For reliable up-to-date information about registration, dog shows and other canine competitions, contact one of the national registries by mail or via the Internet.
American Kennel Club
5580 Centerview Dr., Raleigh, NC 27606-3390
www.akc.org

United Kennel Club
100 E. Kilgore Road, Kalamazoo, MI 49002
www.ukcdogs.com

Canadian Kennel Club
89 Skyway Ave., Suite 100, Etobicoke, Ontario M9W 6R4, Canada
www.ckc.ca

The Kennel Club
1-5 Clarges St., Piccadilly, London W1Y 8AB, UK
www.the-kennel-club.org.uk

your way up" part that you must keep in mind.

Assuming that you have purchased a puppy of the correct type and quality for showing, let's begin to examine the world of showing and what's required to get started. Although the entry fee into a dog show is nominal, there are lots of other hidden costs involved with "finishing" your Gordon Setter, that is, making him a champion. Things like equipment, travel, training and conditioning all cost money. A more serious campaign will include fees for a professional handler, boarding, cross-country travel and advertising. Top-winning show dogs can represent a very considerable investment—over $100,000 has been spent in campaigning some dogs. (The investment can be less,

Showing off his Scottish heritage, this Gordon performs a heelwork routine while wearing his favorite kilt. Heelwork is a relatively new competitive sport in which dog and handler perform to music.

Success in the show ring requires more than a pretty face, a waggy tail and a pocketful of liver. Even though dog shows can be exciting and enjoyable, the sport of conformation makes great demands on the exhibitors and the dogs. Winning exhibitors live for their dogs, devoting time and money to their dogs' presentation, conditioning and training. Very few novices, even those with good dogs, will find themselves in the winners' circle, though it does happen. Don't be disheartened, though. Every exhibitor began as a novice and worked his way up to the Group ring. It's the "working

Ch. Brentwood's Dimpled Chad, shown winning BIS at Sacramento Valley Dog Fanciers Association in 2004, handled by Eileen Hackett for owners C. & P. Krothe.

Madison Square Garden, and the victorious dog becomes a celebrity overnight.

AKC CONFORMATION BASICS

Visiting a dog show as a spectator is a great place to start. Pick up the show catalog to find out what time your breed is being shown, who is judging the breed and in which ring the classes will be held. To start, Gordon Setters compete against other Gordon Setters, and the winner is selected as Best of Breed by the judge. This is the procedure for each breed. At a group show, all of the Best of Breed winners go on to compete for Group One (first place) in their respective groups. For example, all Best of Breed winners in a given group compete against each other; this is done for all seven

of course, for owners who don't use professional handlers.)

Many owners, on the other hand, enter their "average" Gordon Setters in dog shows for the fun and enjoyment of it. Dog showing makes an absorbing hobby, with many rewards for dogs and owners alike. If you're having fun, meeting other people who share your interests and enjoying the overall experience, you likely will catch the "bug." Once the dog-show bug bites, its effects can last a lifetime; it's certainly much better than a deer tick! Soon you will be envisioning yourself in the center ring at the Westminster Kennel Club Dog Show in New York City, competing for the prestigious Best in Show cup. This magical dog show is televised annually from

BECOMING A CHAMPION

An official AKC championship of record requires that a dog accumulate 15 points under three different judges, including two "majors" under different judges. Points are awarded based on the number of dogs entered into competition, varying from breed to breed and place to place. A win of three, four or five points is considered a "major." The AKC annually assigns a schedule of points to adjust to the variations that accompany a breed's popularity and the population of a given area.

FIVE CLASSES AT SHOWS

At most AKC all-breed shows, there are five regular classes offered: Puppy, Novice, Bred-by-Exhibitor, American-bred and Open. The Puppy Class is usually divided as 6 to 9 months of age and 9 to 12 months of age. When deciding in which class to enter your dog, whether male or female, you must carefully check the show schedule to make sure that you have selected the right class. Depending on the age of the dog, previous first-place wins and the sex of the dog, you must make the best choice. It is possible to enter a one-year-old dog who has not won sufficient first places in any of the non-Puppy Classes, though the competition is more intense the further you progress from the Puppy Class.

groups. Finally, all seven group winners go head to head in the ring for the Best in Show award.

What most spectators don't understand is the basic idea of conformation. A dog show is often referred as a "conformation" show. This means that the judge should decide how each dog stacks up (conforms) to the breed standard for his given breed: how well does this Gordon Setter conform to the ideal representative detailed in the standard? Ideally, this is what happens. In reality, however, this ideal often gets slighted as the judge compares Gordon Setter #1 to Gordon Setter #2. Again, the ideal is that each dog is judged based on his merits in comparison to his breed standard, not in comparison to the other dogs in the ring. It is easier for judges to compare dogs of the same breed to decide which they think is the better specimen; in the Group and Best in Show ring, however, it is very difficult to compare one breed to another, like apples to oranges. Thus the dog's conformation to the breed standard—not to mention advertising dollars and good handling—is essential to success in conformation shows. The dog described in the standard (the standard for each AKC breed is written and approved by the breed's national parent club and then submitted to the AKC for approval) is the perfect dog of that breed, and breeders keep their eye on the standard when they choose which dogs to breed, hoping to get closer

Watching at ringside, waiting for their turn, this Gordon and handler seem calm and relaxed.

SHOW POTENTIAL

How possible is it to predict how your ten-week-old puppy will eventually do in the show ring? Most show dogs reach their prime at around three years of age, when their bodies are physically mature and their coats are in "full bloom." Experienced breeders, having watched countless pups grow into Best of Breed winners, recognize the glowing attributes that spell "show potential." When selecting a puppy for show, it's best to trust the breeder to recommend which puppy will best suit your aspirations. Some breeders recommend starting with a male puppy, which likely will be more "typey" than his female counterpart.

and closer to the ideal with each litter.

Another good first step for the novice is to join a dog club. You will be astonished by the many and different kinds of dog clubs in the country, with about 5,000 clubs holding events every year. Most clubs require that prospective new members present two letters of recommendation from existing members. Perhaps you've made some friends visiting a show held by a particular club and you would like to join that club. Dog clubs may specialize in a single breed, like a local or regional Gordon Setter club, or in a specific pursuit, such as obedience, tracking or hunting tests. There are all-breed clubs for all dog enthusiasts; they sponsor special training days, seminars on topics like grooming or handling or lectures on breeding or canine genetics. There are also clubs that specialize in certain types of dogs, like hunting dogs, herding dogs, companion dogs, etc.

A parent club is the national organization, sanctioned by the AKC, which promotes and safeguards its breed in the US. The Gordon Setter Club of America was formed in 1924 and can be contacted on the Internet at http://gsca.org. The parent club holds an annual national specialty show, usually in a different city each year, in which many of the country's top dogs, handlers and breeders gather to compete. At a specialty show, only members of a single breed are invited to participate. There are also group specialties, in which all members of a group are invited. For more information about dog clubs in your area, contact the AKC at www.akc.org on the Internet or write them at their Raleigh, NC address.

OTHER TYPES OF COMPETITION

In addition to conformation shows, the AKC holds a variety of other competitive events. Obedience trials, agility trials and tracking trials are open to all breeds, while hunting tests, field trials, lure coursing, herding tests and trials, earthdog tests and coonhound events are limited to specific breeds or groups of breeds. The Junior Showmanship program is offered to aspiring young handlers and their dogs, and the Canine Good Citizen® Program is an all-around good-behavior test open to all dogs, pure-bred and mixed.

OBEDIENCE TRIALS

Mrs. Helen Whitehouse Walker, a Standard Poodle fancier, can be credited with introducing obedience trials to the United States. In the 1930s she designed a series of exercises based on those of the Associated Sheep, Police, Army Dog Society of Great

Britain. These exercises were intended to evaluate the working relationship between dog and owner. Since those early days of the sport in the US, obedience trials have grown more and more popular, and now more than 2,000 trials each year attract over 100,000 dogs and their owners. Any dog registered with the AKC, regardless of neutering or other disqualifications that would preclude entry in conformation competition, can participate in obedience trials.

There are three levels of difficulty in obedience competition. The first (and easiest) level is the Novice, in which dogs can earn the Companion Dog (CD) title. The intermediate level is the Open level, in which the Companion Dog Excellent (CDX) title is awarded. The advanced level is the Utility level, in which dogs compete for the Utility Dog

A show dog must learn to stand, or "stack" well, meaning that he stands in such a way to look his best.

performing a recall (or come), long sit and long down and standing for examination. In the Open level, the Novice-level exercises are required again, but this time without a leash and for longer durations. In addition, the dog must clear a broad jump, retrieve over a jump and drop on recall. In the Utility level, the exercises are quite difficult, including executing basic commands based on hand signals, following a complex heeling pattern, locating articles based on scent discrimination and completing jumps at the handler's direction.

Once he's earned the UD title, a dog can go on to win the prestigious title of Utility Dog Excellent (UDX) by winning "legs" in ten shows. Additionally, Utility Dogs who win "legs" in Open B and Utility B earn points toward the lofty title of Obedience Trial Champion (OTCh.). Established in 1977 by the AKC, this title requires a dog to earn 100 points as well as three first places in a combination of Open B and Utility B classes under three different judges. The "brass ring" of obedience competition is the AKC's National Obedience Invitational. This is an exclusive competition for only the cream of the obedience crop. In order to qualify for the invitational, a dog must be ranked in either the top 25 all-breeds in obedience or in the top three for his breed in

Every dog in the ring gets a hands-on evaluation from the judge. Artful grooming or posing can hide faults, but the judge's exam doesn't lie!

(UD) title. Classes at each level are further divided into "A" and "B," with "A" for beginners and "B" for those with more experience. In order to win a title at a given level, a dog must earn three "legs." A "leg" is accomplished when a dog scores 170 or higher (200 is a perfect score). The scoring system gets a little trickier when you understand that a dog must score more than 50% of the points available for each exercise in order to actually earn the points. Available points for each exercise range between 20 and 40.

A dog must complete different exercises at each level of obedience. The Novice exercises are the easiest, with the Open and finally the Utility levels progressing in difficulty. Examples of Novice exercises are on- and off-lead heeling, a figure-8 pattern, obedience. The title at stake here is that of National Obedience Champion (NOC).

AGILITY TRIALS

Agility trials became sanctioned by the AKC in August 1994, when the first licensed agility trials were held. Since that time, agility certainly has grown in popularity by leaps and bounds, literally! The AKC allows all registered breeds (including Miscellaneous Class breeds) to participate, providing the dog is 12 months of

GORDONS IN OBEDIENCE

George Dixon and his spectacular dog named Ch. Timberdoodle Dan of Avalon set the bar for Gordons in obedience—unfortunately, he set it rather high! Dan won his UDT (as well as his show championship) in 1941 and was the first (and only) Gordon to win both titles. As history has it, the first three Gordons to win a CD degree were Barnage Highland Chloe, owned by J.D. Rogers; Ch. Heslop's Burnvale Bonnie, owned by Muriel Clement; and Ch. Wilson's Corrie, owned by Mrs. Vincent Wilcox. By 1958 the first CDX title appeared: Blarneystone's Black Beauty, owned by McGlenn. Since Dan's accomplishment, the first UD degree was claimed by Steelawae Wildfire Weesmokkee in 1972. The first Gordon to win the UD degrees in both the US and Canada was Alistair Meadow Melody, owned by Jan Hofer. She won this in 1980.

age or older. Agility is designed so that the handler demonstrates how well the dog can work at his side. The handler directs his dog through, over, under and around an obstacle course that includes jumps, tires, the dog walk, weave poles, pipe tunnels, collapsed tunnels and more. While working his way through the course, the dog must keep one eye and ear on the handler and the rest of his body on the course. The handler runs along with the dog, giving verbal and hand signals to guide the dog through the course.

The first organization to promote agility trials in the US was the United States Dog Agility Association, Inc. (USDAA). Established in 1986, the USDAA

Ch. Brentwood BMW of Berridale, owned by Chuck Krothe, winning the Gordon Setter Club of America's national specialty in 2001 from the Veteran Class.

Ch. Rockaplenty's Run For The Roses, shown winning the Gordon Setter Club of America specialty in Colorado in 1982, handled by Marilyn Title.

sparked the formation of many member clubs around the country. To participate in USDAA trials, dogs must be at least 18 months of age.

The USDAA and AKC both offer titles to winning dogs, although the exercises and requirements of the two organizations differ. Agility Dog (AD), Advanced Agility Dog (AAD) and Master Agility Dog (MAD) are the titles offered by the USDAA, while the AKC offers Novice Agility (NA), Open Agility (OA), Agility Excellent (AX) and Master

JUNIOR SHOWMANSHIP

For budding dog handlers, ages 10 to 18 years, Junior Showmanship competitions are an excellent training ground for the next generation of dog professionals. Owning and caring for a dog are wonderful methods of teaching children responsibility, and Junior Showmanship builds upon that foundation. Juniors learn by grooming, handling and training their dogs, and the quality of a junior's presentation of the dog (and himself) is evaluated by a licensed judge. The junior can enter with any registered AKC dog to compete, including an Indefinite Listing Privilege, provided that the dog lives with him or a member of his family.

Junior Showmanship competitions are divided into two classes: Novice (for beginners) and Open (for juniors who have three first place wins in the Novice Class). The junior must run with the dog with the rest of the handlers and dogs, stack the dog for examination and individually gait the dog in a specific pattern. Juniors should practice with a handling class or an experienced handler before entering the Novice Class so that they recognize all the jargon that the judge may use.

A National Junior Organization was founded in 1997 to help promote the sport of dog showing among young people. The AKC also offers a Junior Scholarship for juniors who excel in the program.

Agility Excellent (MX). Beyond these four AKC titles, dogs can win additional titles in "jumper" classes: Jumper with Weave Novice (NAJ), Open (OAJ) and Excellent (MXJ). The ultimate title in AKC agility is MACH, Master Agility Champion. Dogs can continue to add number designations to the MACH title, indicating how many times the dog has met the title's requirements (MACH1, MACH2 and so on).

Agility trials are a great way to keep your dog active, and they will keep you running, too! You should join a local agility club to learn more about the sport. These clubs offer sessions in which you can introduce your dog to the various obstacles as well as training classes to prepare him for competition. In no time, your dog will be climbing A-frames, crossing the dog walk and flying over hurdles, all with you right beside him. Your heart will leap every time your dog jumps through the hoop—and you'll be having just as much (if not more) fun!

TRACKING

Tracking tests are exciting ways to test your Gordon Setter's instinctive scenting ability on a competitive level. All dogs have a nose, and all breeds are welcome in tracking tests. The first AKC-licensed tracking test took place in 1937 as part of the Utility level at an obedience trial, and thus

competitive tracking was officially begun. The first title, Tracking Dog (TD), was offered in 1947, ten years after the first official tracking test. It was not until 1980 that the AKC added the title Tracking Dog Excellent (TDX), which was followed by the title Versatile Surface Tracking (VST) in 1995. Champion Tracker (CT) is awarded to a dog who has earned all three of those titles.

The TD level is the first and most basic level in tracking, progressing in difficulty to the TDX and then the VST. A dog must follow a track laid by a human 30 to 120 minutes prior in order to earn the TD title. The track is about 500 yards long and contains up to 5 directional changes. At the next level, the TDX, the dog must follow a 3- to 5-hour-old track over a course that

One type of conformation show is the benched show, which provides designated areas for the dogs to rest while not being exhibited.

is up to 1,000 yards long and has up to 7 directional changes. In the most difficult level, the VST, the

ON THE MOVE

The truest test of a dog's proper structure is his gait, the way the dog moves. The American Kennel Club defines gait as "the pattern of footsteps at various rates of speed, each pattern distinguished by a particular rhythm and footfall." That the dog moves smoothly and effortlessly indicates to the judge that the dog's structure is well made. From the four-beat gallop, the fastest of canine gaits, to the high-lifting hackney gait, each breed varies in its correct gait; not every breed is expected to move in the same way. Each breed standard defines the correct gait for its breed and often identifies movement faults, such as toeing in, side-winding, over-reaching or crossing over.

track is up to five hours old and located in an urban setting.

FIELD TRIALS

Field trials are offered to the retrievers, pointers and spaniel breeds of the Sporting Group as well as to the Beagles, Dachshunds and Bassets of the Hound Group. The purpose of field trials is to demonstrate a dog's ability to perform his breed's original purpose in the field. The events vary depending on the type of dog, but in all trials dogs compete against one another for placement and for points toward their Field Champion (FC) title. Dogs that earn their FC title plus their championship in the conformation ring are known as Dual Champions; this is extremely prestigious, as it shows that the dog is the ideal blend of form and function, excelling in both areas.

Retriever field trials, designed to simulate "an ordinary day's shoot," are popular and likely the most demanding of these trials. Dogs must "mark" the location of downed feathered game and then return the birds to the shooter. Successful dogs are able to "mark" the downed game by remembering where the bird fell as well as correct use of the wind and terrain. Dogs are tested both on land and in water.

Difficulty levels are based on the number of birds downed as well as the number of "blind retrieves" (where a bird is placed away from the view of the dog and the handler directs the dog by the use of hand signals and verbal commands). The term "Non-Slip" retriever, often applied to these trials, refers to a dog that is steady at the handler's side until commanded to go. Every field trial includes four stakes of increasing levels of difficulty. Each stake is judged by a team of two judges who look for many natural abilities, including steadiness, courage, style, control and training.

HUNTING TESTS

Hunting tests are not competitive like field trials, and participating dogs are judged against a standard, as in a conformation show. The first hunting tests were devised by the North American Hunting Retriever Association (NAHRA) as an alternative to field trials for retriever owners to appreciate their dogs' natural innate ability in the field without the expense and pressure of a formal field trial. The intent of hunting tests is the same as that of field trials: to test the dog's ability in a simulated hunting scenario.

The AKC instituted its hunting tests in June 1985; since then, their popularity has grown tremendously. The AKC offers three titles at hunting tests, Junior Hunter (JH), Senior Hunter (SH) and Master Hunter (MH). Each title requires that the dog earn

qualifying "legs" at the tests: the JH requiring four; the SH, five; and the MH, six. In addition to the AKC, the United Kennel Club also offers hunting tests through its affiliate club, the Hunting Retriever Club, Inc. (HRC), which began the tests in 1984.

CANINE GOOD CITIZEN® PROGRAM

Have you ever considered getting your dog "certified"? The AKC's Canine Good Citizen® Program affords your dog just that opportunity. Your dog shows that he is a well-behaved canine citizen, using the basic training and good manners you have taught him, by taking a series of ten tests that illustrate that he can behave properly at home, in a public place and around other dogs. The tests are administered by participating dog clubs, colleges, 4-H clubs, Scouts and other community groups and are open to all pure-bred and mixed-breed dogs. Upon passing the ten tests, the suffix CGC is then applied to your dog's name.

The ten tests are: 1. Accepting a friendly stranger; 2. Sitting politely for petting; 3. Appearance and grooming; 4. Walking on a lead; 5. Walking through a group of people 6. Sit, down and stay on command; Coming when called; 8. Meeting another dog; 9. Calm reaction to distractions; 10. Separation from owner.

INDEX

My Gordon Setter

PUT YOUR PUPPY'S FIRST PICTURE HERE

Dog's Name _____

Date _____ Photographer _____